THE
GRADUATE
BIBLE

EMMA VITES

TABLE OF CONTENTS

"This book is dedicated to Nicholas and Geraldine Vites, my inspirational parents who taught me to always be the best version of myself and strive to help others. May you rest in Peace dad"

PROLOGUE

I will never forget the day I received a call from a father who'd found me on the Internet for my career coaching services. He told me his son was really struggling with getting a job and the general direction his life was taking and asked if I could help. His son had just left college, didn't have any career aspirations and didn't know what to do. I then went to meet his son and I remember a very shy, quiet young guy sitting in front of me. I asked him what he enjoyed doing best and he said he loved playing video games. He spent all day, every day playing video games. I then asked him one simple question.

"Who do you think would find those skills valuable?"

"No one," he said, with a glum expression on his face.

"Think again," I replied. "There is definitely someone who would find the fact that you have spent eight to ten hours a day testing games valuable." He then mentioned that a gaming company may find those skills valuable. "Exactly!" was my response.

I then helped him develop his social media representation. I asked him to create a blog. Within the blog he would write about every game he played. I asked him to write what he liked about the game, what he didn't like and how it could be improved. We then changed his Twitter handle to read, "Obsessed with everything to do with gaming, seeking a job in the gaming industry as a games tester," and asked him to attach his new blog. He proceeded to follow every CEO of the top gaming companies and also started following the developers who created the games.

The next thing we worked on was his CV He tailored it by enhancing all of his experience working in retail gaming shops and we included a link to his blog. He also updated his LinkedIn profile with the same message: "Passionate about securing a job as a games tester within the gaming industry" and followed relevant companies and people.

Once his new social media profiles were created, we worked on improving his confidence and belief issues about how important his skills would be to a gaming company. I helped him understand how a gaming company makes money and what their priorities are. As per most businesses, a gaming company is interested in making money, saving money and mitigating risk.

- Gaming companies can **make money** by selling more games. The only way to sell more games is to create games that people will buy. This is where his skills were invaluable as he could make suggestions as to which were the best games and what was currently missing in the market.

- Gaming companies can **save money** by not producing overly expensive games, which won't sell as well as cheaper counterparts. Again, his skills were invaluable as he had the experience to pinpoint the strengths in successful games and could advise on which titles that company should concentrate on.

"Once his new social media profiles were created, we worked on improving his confidence and belief issues about how important his skills would be to a gaming company."

- Finally, he could help **mitigate risk** by advising on the games that were likely to be the most successful for them. Furthermore, he could tell those companies what their weaknesses were and how their games could be improved.

Once he started to understand how he could add great value to a gaming company, he aced his interviews and I'm pleased to say he was offered his dream job as a games tester at SEGA!

This story forms the basis to *The Graduate Bible*. Although you may not have years of experience, there are usually skills that you already possess that can add exceptional value to a business.

INTRODUCTION

People often ask me what compelled me to write this book and I respond by saying I had no choice! I wrote this book at a unique time of life.

I had been living in Australia for years working in the field of Graduate recruitment and after a few years, I decided to leave Australia to move back to the UK to be closer to my family. I booked a round the world ticket, so I could spend some time travelling prior to returning to the UK. Unfortunately for me whilst I was travelling, my life was shattered and altered forever. My dad, who was my best friend and biggest influence in my life passed away whilst I was in Bali. I made it home for the funeral and then continued my travels solo around the world for another 10 months. Whilst I was travelling, I studied meditation and mindfulness to help me cope with my grief. I met teachers every step of the way in Peru, Bolivia, Brazil, Argentina, SE Asia and Europe. By the time my travels were coming to an end, I had a compelling urge to write down my knowledge of my previous 8+ years graduate recruitment experience to help as many people as I could. My dad was a doctor and philanthropist and spent his life saving people's lives and helping others and I wanted to do the same. The information kept flowing out of me and I had no choice but to write it down.

It was this drive and desire to help people that also led me to set up my company, 'The Apprentice Project' (www.theapprenticeproject.com), which exists today as an educational resource and coaching company helping young people live their best lives and land their dream job.

The background...

During my 8+ years working in Graduate recruitment in the UK and Australia, I noticed that only a tiny percentage of the graduates who applied through our process were successful. I was involved in running weekly assessment centres to find the *crème de la crème* of graduates, yet from the 500 initial applicants, only 5 got though! That means we were rejecting 495 graduates every week! Most of these candidates didn't receive feedback and I was shocked by the lack of available resources explaining where they were going wrong, and how they could improve and become the people employers want them to be.

You've spent lots of money and years of your time on your education, and it is now important to channel your energies into what employers are looking for. This includes how to write the perfect CV/resume, how to perform in an interview, how to ace an assessment centre and how to communicate effectively so that you can put all your hard work and effort to good use.

The most apparent problem I noticed was the lack of focus most graduates have. Most of you are clueless as to which careers even exist and therefore you simply don't know what to do! This causes the greatest challenge, because employers are only interested in hiring graduates who know what they want and demonstrate a clear passion for the role they are applying to. Michael Acton Smith, CEO of calm.com and Mind Candy (*Moshi Monsters*) told me that, "The two things that he looks for are passion and focus," and this seemed to be the case across the board with all of the employers I interviewed for this book.

I remember when I finished university that there was a distinct lack of resources telling me what to do next. Now I feel the times have changed and, with the rise of the internet, there is almost too much information available. However there is still no information telling you how to be what employers want you to be. You know you have to be 'confident', but what does that even mean? And how can you improve your confidence? What tools and techniques can you use? My motto is: "You don't know what you don't know, but you can learn…"

Something else most career books neglect to mention is that you are not interviewing with a company, you are interviewing with a person – so this book teaches you how to communicate with all types of people. I studied psychology at university and during my travels, I studied to become a Master NLP (Neuro-Linguistic Programming) practitioner, IMA practitioner and emotional intelligence coach, and therefore I have incorporated all of these techniques into this book to help you make a great first impression.

I have worked across 3 continents in amazing cities including New York, San Francisco, Sydney, Melbourne and London and have included insights into what employers are looking for globally within this book.

I have also had the privilege of working for LinkedIn for 5+ years, which is the world's largest professional network. LinkedIn is the no1 place recruiters and employers look for talent and within this book you learn how to fill out your LinkedIn profile in the most effective way and how to get a job within the 'hidden job market'.

If you use this practical guide step by step, it really will become your job-seeking bible!

Emma Vites, BA

CHAPTER 1: ON GRADUATING

FURTHER EDUCATION NEEDS TO START ... AT SCHOOL!

Read the news and you will quickly be reminded that youth unemployment is a global problem. With rising tuition fees and a perceived lack of key skills amongst the global young workplace – there has never been a greater need to develop and harness the enterprise and talent of today's graduates.

I don't know about you but as much as I loved school, I'm still convinced that half of what I studied was irrelevant for the 'real world'. I can pretty much guarantee that my years studying Latin or Pythagoras theorem have not enriched me in my adult life or my career.

If the whole point of school was to get into university and the whole point of university was to get a good career, then why were subjects such as 'how to prepare for future life' or 'how to get a good career' left out of the school curriculum? Could we not have replaced Religious Education with 'communicating and understanding different cultures in life and business'? Or how about replacing Latin with Business? Maths should have included accountancy, investment and tax, and the sciences could have incorporated Philosophy to help us explain the universal laws of nature. Rather than spending time on 'general studies', why on earth weren't we being taught how to sell ourselves in life and business?

Can you imagine if we all left school with a clear picture of which careers existed and what we needed to do to succeed in business and in life? Our communication skills would improve, we would be better equipped to handle life's challenges and we would be able to 'sell' ourselves more effectively, which, let's face it, is the key to being successful in this world. We would also encourage more young entrepreneurs and this would be a brilliant engine for growth in our economy.

I was lucky enough to be exposed to the Young Enterprise scheme at school, where we were encouraged to create a company and produce products and services to sell to the public. The scheme's mission statement is "to inspire and equip young people to learn and succeed through enterprise". What I want to know is why Young Enterprise wasn't compulsory? Surely teaching children the lessons of business at a young age would be vital for their future career success?

I am very confused by the education system and wonder why these vital changes haven't been made. During my career in graduate recruitment and after speaking to thousands of employers, they all say the same thing about the competencies they are looking for when they recruit. Candidates have to be self-confident and have high levels of verbal communication skills. They need to be driven and dynamic, and have the ability to influence and persuade. They also have to have a high level of structure and logic. If these are the skills and competencies needed to succeed in life and business, then why aren't we being taught how to improve on these areas at school?

My preferred school curriculum would include personality profiling so that teachers could understand how to best communicate with each child (teach in the student's language and map of the world) and utilise visual, kinaesthetic and auditory education tools. They would have access to a coach to improve their level of confidence, self-belief and communication skills. They would have lessons in business and Young Enterprise would be a compulsory scheme. They would be taught about saving money, investing, tax and accountancy, and they would have dedicated careers lessons, during which business mentors would be invited in to speak. This would encourage students to pick a career that is right for them, helping them decide whether or not they should go to university.

With these changes implemented I am convinced that unemployment would be reduced, the economy would flourish and grow, and the world would be a more positive place.

Within this book, you will learn all the skills you need to be the people employers want you to be. You will learn about your own personality style and how to adapt to the style of the company you want to work for. You will learn about the hidden job market and how to stand out from the crowd. More importantly you will see how your lack of experience can add tremendous value to a company.

A SHORTAGE OF THE RIGHT SKILLS...

There has been a shift in employer's perception of the job market, where they now believe there is an abundance of candidates looking for work and this has put employers in a 'position of power'. Employers are becoming fussier when hiring, demanding candidates who will add value, who will build networks, who will help them grow and who will be an asset to their business. The challenge for graduates is overcoming this high expectation!

In the past, employers didn't have the luxury of cherry-picking the top talent. It was very much a candidates' market – they could pick and choose where to work, leaving organisations with no choice but to headhunt the top talent from their competitors for an expensive fee. Now the tables have turned as employers enjoy their new 'position of power', fully expecting to pick and choose the best of the best.

This is especially challenging for you as graduates, as there isn't the luxury of experience to lean on; it all has to do with your personality.

So how can you become the best of the best? How can you be the person employers want to hire? How can you stand out from the crowd? As I mentioned earlier, the first point to remember is that the company you want to work for is in business to make money, save money and mitigate risk, so you need to position yourself in a way that you can add value in at least one of those areas.

Also it is important to remember a brief lesson I learnt whilst studying psychology. The person who is interviewing you has an ego. It is vital to stroke this ego by explaining to them that this is the company you want to work for and nothing else will do. You want to learn from that person alone and be a part of their team and business – and no one else's!

The more focused you are on what you want, the more likely you will get a job in your chosen profession. I recently placed a graduate really quickly purely because he said he only wanted to work for a 'green energy consultancy' company. This made

"The person who is interviewing you has an ego. It is vital to stroke this ego by explaining to them that this is the company you want to work for and nothing else will do."

my job as a recruiter much easier as I only focused on getting him a job in that particular industry. Of course this impressed his new employer because the graduate was so passionate and informed about the industry. He clearly demonstrated his value and it worked.

The best news is that having no experience is often more appealing to an employer (especially a dynamic, fast growth, entrepreneurial company) than someone with experience, as they will be seeking people who can be moulded into their company culture with no pre-conceptions or bad habits. They will want to target a new, younger generation – which is perfect for the graduate age group – and they won't want to pay for costly, experienced people who may or may not work out. So use this to your advantage and start studying your own strengths and thinking about how you can add value today.

HOW TO APPLY TOP SALES SKILLS TO GETTING A JOB

One of the reasons many of you find it challenging to get a job is because you generally have no idea how to 'sell' yourselves in an interview situation. You are unaware of the value you can bring companies, as you are constantly hearing from employers that they want 'experience only'. Compounding this, the recession has meant that there is now a significantly larger proportion of experienced people on the market.

After a fantastic career as a top Sales performer across many industries including Marketing, Software, Recruitment and Training, I have realised that the same skills that made me successful as a salesperson are the exact same skills you need to get a job. An interview is a place for you to sell yourself to a potential employer.

To be successful, there is an 'art' and a 'science' to the profession of Sales. The 'art' includes possessing all the competencies required to be successful, which at its basic level boils down to people skills. The 'science' is the exciting part. There are certain tools and techniques that you can use for selling anything, including yourself, such as building rapport, asking effective questions, presentation techniques, networking techniques, closing techniques, etc.

For Sales people and graduates alike, I have also noticed there is another layer of tools and techniques that can be used across all industries. These include:

1. Understand how business works

All CEOs want to grow their business and be profitable. As we have already discussed, they will only invest in products and services that make them money, save them money or mitigate risk. This includes 'talent'. Therefore you need to position yourself and communicate how to highlight these points. For example, when I used to work in graduate recruitment and I was selling the best graduates for junior level sales positions, I would say to my clients that I would help them:

a) **Make money** – "I only select the best graduates in the country who possess the competencies needed to successfully make sales for your business and therefore maximise the revenue of your company."

b) **Save money** – "Hiring graduates is considerably more cost effective than hiring costly, experienced sales people."

c) **Mitigate risk** – "I train graduates using a proven method that teaches them to cold-call, book meetings, generate leads and CLOSE. I also use proven personality profiling tools to get the best matches in the first place."

When it becomes about you 'selling yourself' an example could be:

a) **Make money** – "I find it really easy to meet and speak to new people. This was highlighted during my gap year when I managed to navigate travelling the world on my own. This means I have the confidence and networking skills to promote your business, which will result in new business and referrals, which will increase the revenue of your business."

b) **Save money** – "As a new graduate I am looking for an opportunity to showcase the skills I developed during my time at university and I will be a much more affordable option than an experienced person. This means I will save your business money."

c) **Mitigate risk** – "Many experienced people will have picked up bad habits from their previous employers and may have formed negative preconceptions about the role and your company. I have no negative preconceptions and can be moulded into the star performer you want me to be."

2. Understand your client's business

If you can talk confidently in an interview about developments in the industry, then you will be in a stronger position to sell yourself as a candidate. This is easy. When I'm selling to a marketing director, I read *MarketingWeek* and attend marketing events. When I'm selling to a software company, I read *Computerworld* and follow Twitter, LinkedIn and Google alerts to keep me up to date with the latest changes. I also scan every potential customer's website to understand what they do, who they sell to and what their business objectives are.

You should apply these classic sales techniques to an interview situation. The more prepared you are, the better you will do.

3. Understand people

Always remember you are never talking to a company; you are talking to a person. Many people forget this and miss out a crucial human element. With the rise of social media, especially LinkedIn, it is now very easy to understand more about the people you are targeting, which will help with building rapport (often the most crucial part of the interview process). If you can discuss topics of interest to the people you are meeting and speak to them in the way they would most appreciate, then you stand a far greater chance of getting hired.

There are four main language styles that people communicate with and later in this book I will guide you through a personality/ language profiling questionnaire via ima-connecting.com to find out more about your preferred language style and how you can adapt your communication to suit others.

But for now, I would like to congratulate you on your graduation, and welcome you with open arms into the business world. Now, where are all those jobs?

CHAPTER 2: READY, GET SET ... GO!

You've just graduated, now what do you do?

You need to find the best career for you.

But what do jobs mean? Where do you start?

Securing a job is just like an art.

There are ways to act and research to do

And reading this book will give you a clue

It's not easy being a graduate. You have just spent three or four years (sometimes more) in education and then you find yourself in the big, wide world looking for a job. Suddenly you realise you are competing with thousands of other graduates in exactly the same position! So how do you make yourself stand out? What tips are there to ensure you get a job before your peers? Luckily here I have all the answers for you.

Firstly, please remember that although what you have studied is important and good grades help when it comes to getting a job, employers aren't interested in grades; they are interested in the personal qualities within you. Therefore being social, energetic, positive, hard-working, presentable and likable are going to be more important than getting an 'A' in an essay. Obviously this is all dependent on the role you are searching for – for example, a doctor or a lawyer needs to get the top grades – but what if you are competing against another graduate with exactly the same grades? Then what do employers look for? YES! Your *personality*.

A great example of this was a candidate called Richard who left school with three Ds at A-level and a 2:2 in his degree. Now on the surface, you wouldn't think he would be immediately successful on the career ladder, except he left university with not one, but three job offers! So how did he do it? Richard did what most other graduates fail to do and that was being incredibly proactive at university. He was the leader of the Enterprise Society, he started an organisation called Young, Black and Successful, he joined loads of societies, wrote articles, utilised social media and generally made a name for himself. He left with job offers in PR, at a major investment bank and for a government organisation.

This proves that employers are looking for graduates who can add value to their organisation by being proactive, and by being willing to work hard and go the extra mile. These are the competencies employers seek and it is these skills I will teach you in this book.

BE FOUR STEPS AHEAD OF YOUR COMPETITION

Universities understand the need to push employability and that is because they need to justify their expensive fees. I am a big believer in learning and studying and, as the great Stephen Covey says, you need to "begin with the end in mind".

It is vital that you know where you are heading, so you can map out how to get there. You can break it down simply. What do you like doing? Think about what skills you have that other people don't. Are you sociable? Are you friendly? Do you find starting conversations with strangers easy? Do you enjoy growing your social media network? Then perhaps a client or customer-facing role would suit you. Are you the friend who organises all the nights out? Are you always on time and good with money? Perhaps a project management role would suit you, or maybe event management? The list goes on.

Firstly you need to identify your strengths. Once you have done that, start reading dedicated careers books to see what roles exist and also browse LinkedIn to find roles that are appealing to you. The great thing about social media is that all the information about jobs and the people who are in them is there for you to see. Using LinkedIn, you can even connect with these professionals and ask for help, or follow key influencers to see what their advice is. The web has transformed your job search.

BUT WHAT IF EMPLOYERS REQUIRE PREVIOUS EXPERIENCE?

"In determining the right people, the good-to-great companies placed greater weight on character attributes than on specific educational background, practical skills, specialised knowledge, or work experience."
Jim Collins – business consultant, author and lecturer

It is my belief that graduates, given access to the 'right' training, can add just as much value to a role as experienced and seasoned professionals. So how can you start selling yourself against older candidates with more experience?

Here are my top five tips:

1. Experience is great and very valuable if it is found in a person with a proven track record of success and a positive attitude. However, as a result of the current market, many experienced people have now found themselves on the job market and are upset and angry about their situation. This negative energy is transferred from one job to another

and they will want to be paid more for the privilege. What you can offer a company is a complete blank canvas, free from negative preconceptions or bad habits formed from previous experience, meaning they can mould you into the way they would like. This positive energy and beginning to your role is crucial for business success.

2. As mentioned above, experienced people require a larger salary when beginning a new job. They have more commitments. They may be married, have kids, a mortgage, etc. The benefit of a company hiring *you* is that you are often free from such commitments and are therefore a much more affordable solution, especially in this current marketplace.

3. Graduates and young people in general have been introduced to different technologies at a more rapid rate than more mature, experienced candidates. This means that you can adapt to change, can assimilate information faster and can bring an organisation to the forefront of their industry more quickly.

4. Having recently been to college or university, you are still in 'learning mode'. Most experienced people quit their quest to learn a long time ago. Their egos may have got in the way and a 'know it all' attitude may have formed. You as graduates are used to learning and can therefore assimilate a company's product line very quickly, easily picking up methodologies.

5. Graduates have been more exposed to social media, which is a powerful marketing tool for most companies and a very valuable asset. You also know how to communicate to a younger audience, which again is a prized asset for most organisations.

The biggest resistance most employers have against taking on graduates is the amount of time they will have to spend training you on the skills they need. They rely on experienced people to just 'come in and get the job done'. I advise any graduate to undertake the following prior to any interview or job application:

- Work shadow or intern with somebody who is doing your desired job right now, so you have some level of understanding and prior experience to bring to an interview.

- Research the company or companies for which you wish to work (Use LinkedIn). Your research should centre on their growth objectives and their best products or services. Following that, compile a SWOT analysis for the company (covering Strengths, Weaknesses, Opportunities and Threats) and examine how you want to help them become a market leader (if appropriate). Think about potential value you can bring.

- Demonstrate that you are a quick learner. Think of examples and have them ready to introduce in an interview. These examples now become your 'selling points'.

FINDING A JOB

Make no mistake – finding a job is a job in itself. You are now an entrepreneur with a mission to accomplish. As you focus on your goals ahead, prepare your environment by making it conducive to concentration and create a work area within your home that is devoted to your search. Get into a routine and follow it each day. Imagine yourself as a salesperson: you must sniff out leads and make useful contacts. If you come across a company you particularly want to work for, then be brave – call them or email them and request an informational interview.

You will go through ups and downs, have good days and bad days, but the more you keep practising, the better prepared you will be for interviews and assessment days.

Remember, it's important always to be realistic, especially during a recession. Here are some realities to bear in mind:

Reality 1 – The average job search is several months, sometimes longer. Many companies are cutting back, meaning HR departments are understaffed and overworked.

Reality 2 – Don't just send out a generic CV/resume. The content of your CV and the approach to distributing it is paramount to your success. You will need to network and contact companies.

Reality 3 – Focusing is good but not if it is on a struggling industry with little growth. Be prepared to rethink your goals.

Reality 4 – Be wary of any job that seems too good to be true, because it probably is. If you're being promised a 'get rich quick' scheme, you feel pressured to make a decision, or someone is requesting payment of any kind, then be cautious.

Reality 5 – No one cares about you, it is all about what you can do for them. Sorry.

"Don't just rely on job boards to find a job. Not all openings are posted. Become that salesperson, send an email or inmail on LinkedIn and then make a call introducing yourself."

Reality 6 – Don't just rely on job boards to find a job. Not all openings are posted. Become that salesperson, send an email or inmail on LinkedIn and then make a call introducing yourself.

Reality 7 – The more personal your approach, the better off you will be. Dealing with people directly is always preferable.

Reality 8 – Even if you strongly suspect you have been successful at interview, keep applying for jobs until you receive a formal letter of offer.

Firstly though, before potential employers even get to experience your drive and personality at interview stage, you need to write a decent CV!

CHAPTER 3: THE ART OF WRITING A CV

All employers want to see is

A piece of paper called a CV

They need to know what you have done

To see if you're their 'chosen one'.

But what if you have no experience, what do you write?

Especially if you haven't done much with your life!

You went to university and that was it,

So how do you add value bit by bit?

In this chapter, I'll show you how,

So relax and breathe and get started now!

Writing a CV can be a scary experience. All of your hard work at university has to be summarised on a few pieces of paper, and this is the only tool employers have for making a decision whether to put you in the 'yes' or the 'no' pile.

Firstly, employers give you a LOT of clues about what they are looking for. Let's examine the following example:

GRADUATE ENTRY-LEVEL BUSINESS DEVELOPMENT – EVENTS COMPANY

Our client specialises in providing professional speakers, entertainers and business facilitators throughout the UK. They work hand in hand with companies to understand their requirements to make events and conferences stand out from the rest. They are looking for an entry-level business development person to generate new business opportunities and work on client account management.

The management team with whom you will be working closely has over 20 years' experience within the industry. Their knowledge and business systems will be provided to you to ensure your success in this role. The team is currently made up of seven long-standing team members, which is a testament to the way the company is run. The office environment is very relaxed and funky, in line with the industry.

In order to succeed in this position the right person will have relevant experience in:

* Creative proposal writing

* Great attention to detail

* A displayed passion for speaking and conferences

* Broad general knowledge would be favourable in media, sport, business and personalities

* Great communicator

Although our client has a list of current clients that have been associated with the company for many years, there will be an element of cold calling to particular people and companies in order to enhance and further your position.

The owner is prepared to reward the right person according to his/her experience. You will be remunerated with a retainer plus commission based on a realistic, achievable structure. There will also be times when you will have to entertain and attend client functions.

As you can see from the above example, they tell you *exactly* what they are looking for! 'Creative proposal writing, great attention to detail, a passion for speaking and conferences, broad general knowledge in media, sport, business and personalities and a great communicator.'

Therefore now all you would do is write examples of where you have demonstrated each of those skills.

For example: 'At university I had to write proposals all the time for my course, which has greatly enhanced my proposal-writing skills.'

'A huge part of my degree was submitting creative stories and presentations, providing me with an excellent writing ability that can be utilised for all work-related documentation.'

'I represented my school in all the public speaking competitions in the borough due to my passion for communication and conferences.'

When writing your CV, always include clear examples of how you have demonstrated what they are looking for. The best advice I can provide you comes in the form of three little words:

FEATURE ... PROOF ... BENEFIT
Feature – I have great communication skills

Proof – This is demonstrated by the fact I was chosen to represent my school in all the public speaking competitions across the borough

Benefit – This means I will be able to liaise with decision makers at all levels with ease, both internally and externally

The FEATURE … PROOF … BENEFIT rule is also perfect for interviews (please see Chapter 6).

Many people get confused with the amount of pages you should have in a CV and this can vary according to the role and your level of experience, but one rule of thumb is **employers will search for the buzzwords on Page 1**. This means that you need to begin with a punchy career objective, which relates to their role and their company. I would recommend not having any more than two pages.

So with the example I provided, you would write:

"I am a great communicator who has accumulated plenty of work experience in the media industry. I am looking for an entry-level role where I can create specialised events that meet my client's individual needs. During my industry placement year, I gained experience of dealing with decision makers at all levels in the media and entertainment industry. I have a working knowledge of speakers and conferences, and I have the ability to write effective proposals as well as a drive and passion to win lots of new business."

SUMMARY OF CV WRITING

1. Read the job ad carefully. Pinpoint exactly what the company is looking for and provide examples of where you may have demonstrated each of those points. Tailor your CV for each and every role.

2. Use the FEATURE … PROOF … BENEFIT rule – so, when you write you have 'great communication skills', back this up with an example, explaining what the benefit is for them.

3. Compose an attention-grabbing career objective tailored to the role you want and the company you are applying to. If you want to work in IT, don't write that you enjoy media!

4. Keep it to two pages ... and have everything punchy and relevant on Page 1.

5. Always include contact details and make sure spelling and grammar are 100% correct.

APPLICATION FORM WRITING

Writing a strong application form shares much in common with perfecting your CV It is equally important to:

- Include and repeat the relevant buzzwords important to your potential employer

- Use specific examples to illustrate your experience

- Demonstrate how you will add value

- Demonstrate how you've gone the extra mile and been the best you can be

- Always ensure spelling and grammar are impeccable

The book *The 6 Reasons You'll Get the Job* by Debra Angel MacDougall and Elisabeth Harney Sanders-Park discusses the six qualities that employers are seeking – though they may not even be aware of it – that if you are able to work to your advantage, could make the difference between receiving the job offer and being a 'finalist'. While the qualities themselves are not really new, the book serves as a good reminder to consider how you are demonstrating them to prospective employers. Let's review each quality and consider ways to show that you possess them.

Presentation: Presentation includes appearance, manners, how you speak and write, and even your online profile. All of this will be discussed within *The Graduate Bible*.

Ability: If you are invited to interview, chances are the employer believes you have the ability to do the job. Your challenge will be to articulate that you are better than your competition, and you can do that by providing proof that you can produce results. When you are asked behavioural questions, respond with specific examples that quantify outcomes and accomplishments. Prepare a portfolio, and do a little 'show and tell' while answering questions – visuals make a strong impact, and are more easily remembered than words.

Dependability: Your work history and education will certainly help demonstrate dependability, but don't underestimate the importance of being on time to the interview, and being prepared with extra copies of your CV Solid letters of reference that speak to your dependability will also be useful.

Motivation: A simple but effective way to demonstrate motivation is to thoroughly research the company prior to your interview. Learn their mission, their challenges, their competition, and their goals. In responding to interview questions, and in asking your own questions, speak with the authority of someone who knows and understands the issues and is willing and able to help resolve them.

Attitude: One person I know was invited to interview for a position for which one of the qualifications was 'flexibility'. The day before the interview was scheduled, she got a call telling her it had been rescheduled. When she got to the interview, the room location and the number of people on the committee had changed. Though she didn't know it, this was all part of the plan to test her attitude and willingness to adapt to the changing circumstances.

Fortunately, she cheerfully accepted all the changes, and by demonstrating such a positive attitude, got the job.

Network: Again, think about the organisation's goals and how your own professional network might be a resource in helping you be successful if you are hired for the position. Build and maintain your LinkedIn profile, and refer to your network as appropriate in the interview.

The authors of the book use the acronym PADMAN as a mnemonic to remember these six qualities:

- **P**resentation

- **A**bility

- **D**ependability

- **M**otivation

- **A**ttitude

- **N**etwork

Seeing yourself through employers' eyes brings perspective to your job search and helps you greatly with getting hired.

EMAIL CORRESPONDENCE

Very often you will be required to email agencies, contacts and potential employers. It's vital to bear in mind that emailing in this instance is very different to the way you would normally email your friends. Here are seven points to consider:

1. Always be polite. Use terms like 'Dear' rather than 'Hi', and end by thanking the recipients for their time. As long as

you have a named contact, close with 'Yours sincerely' – if you don't have a named contact (for example if you're writing to 'info@companyname.com'), then close with 'Yours faithfully'.

2. The subject line exists for a reason – use it! Some ideas, depending on where you are in the interview process are 'Interview request..' or 'Further to our meeting..'

3. Keep it brief – it's important to respect the other person's time and effort spent away from work to attend to your query.

4. Frame your message – have a clear objective. What do you want to achieve? Start with the end in mind!

5. Avoid using emotional language.

6. Only ever send to groups with permission.

7. Don't be a comedian – everybody has a slightly different sense of humour, so it would be unwise to introduce comedy until you know the recipient well.

CHAPTER 4: MARKETING YOURSELF

Of course, writing a good CV, application form and accompanying email are only the first steps. While your CV may show promise and flair, how will any prospective employers know that not only do you have a great personality, but that you're looking for a job without a bit of shameless self-promotion? Without putting yourself 'out there', you are limiting your job search to traditional paths that everybody else will be following. Even though you may not realise or indeed benefit from it now, connections made today will have longstanding repercussions throughout the rest of your career.

For those of you feeling bashful, let me explain in more detail. There are some very obvious aspects to your lives that you have grown up with which can now be exploited in new ways to help you network, build a following and sniff out new jobs which are yet to reach public recruitment stage. That's right – I'm talking about social media – the tool that you most likely already use in some way (Facebook, Twitter, Pinterest, LinkedIn, Instagram and so on). This not only has a business equivalent in the form of LinkedIn, but also will be referenced by future employers and can make you valuable leads. Never before has your online personality been so visible and so intrinsic to success in your chosen career. But before we examine that, let's get the basics right.

HOW TO COMMUNICATE

1. Demonstrate a passion for your subject – no matter whether you're talking in person, on the phone or online, be clear about what you care about and why

2. Take responsibility for the way you relate to others

3. Treat each person equally – whether you like it or not, you are always being judged on some level

4. Be attentive and caring – exactly as you would wish to be treated yourself

5. Convey personal warmth – the more approachable you appear, the more opportunities will come your way

Listening is of vital importance during all forms of communication. One of my mantras is that you have two ears and one mouth – use them in that order. This will not only indicate respect but will also allow you to learn. Constantly talking without taking time to listen to others is not only irritating to the speaker, but it limits you, too.

Particularly in the business world, there are three things you should know about people before they talk:

1. They love to hear themselves talk

2. They want to be heard and understood

3. They are drawn to people who listen to them

Helpful suggestions to build on your listening skills include always asking the right kind of questions – who? What? Where? When? How? Furthermore, asking these open-ended questions is a great way to start or continue a conversation, as it allows the other person to respond in full, without restriction or expectation.

Here are some examples of open-ended questions:

Q: Can you tell me a little bit more about your background; HOW did you get to where you are today?

Q: WHAT do you look for when you are hiring new people for your company? Can you see any of those competencies within me?

Q: WHAT do you think is the number one reason for your success?

Although it's generally a good idea to always act like you have understood the other person (meaning you are giving them a chance), if you genuinely don't understand, then don't risk showing yourself up. Sometimes misunderstandings can be cleared up silently by backtracking – repeating what they have said – and there is no loss of face.

> *"It takes two to speak the truth – one to speak and another to hear"*
> **Henry David Thoreau**

A good rule to remember is when you talk, you say only what you know; when you listen, you learn what others know.

TELEPHONE TIPS

Whether you're calling an agency, a new contact or a potential employer on spec, here are some handy tips to bear in mind when you are communicating by phone:

1. Use the other person's name throughout the conversation to hold his or her attention

2. Match your voice volume to the other person's

3. Likewise, reconcile the speed of your speech

4. Conform your speaking rhythm to your partner's

5. Match your energy too – never run the risk of 'bulldozing' over a carefully mannered opponent

6. Aim to keep your sentence lengths and word choices similar to those of the person you're communicating with

Very often as an applicant you might be expected to participate in an interview over the phone, perhaps as a precursor to a face-to-face interview, or in the case of long distance commutes. I will address interviews at length in Chapter 6, but in the meantime here are some tips on how to handle a phone interview:

1. Always use a landline. This is not the time for your mobile reception to go awry.

2. Be prepared in advance – think about what you already know about the organisation and come up with a handful of talking points to help you create the right impression.

3. Keep fully focussed on the discussion – no multitasking allowed!

4. Listen and blend – apply connected listening to whatever is said.

TELEPHONE INTERVIEWS – YOU HAD ME AT 'HELLO'

Remember Renée Zellweger's famous line in the movie *Jerry Maguire* where she says to Tom Cruise, "You had me at 'hello'"? Scientists have now proven that people judge others instantly by their voice alone. "From the first word you hear a person speak, you start to form this impression of the person's personality," explains Phil McAleer, a psychologist at the University of Glasgow, Scotland.

Telephone interviews are a really easy way for companies to see if an applicant has the competencies most employers are looking for. But one thing candidates don't seem to realise is that the employer can make up his or her mind in the first second of the telephone interview. It all comes down to the word 'Hello'!

The way you say 'Hello' is the most important step of a telephone interview. If you sound bored, unexcited, unenthusiastic, distracted or not articulate enough, then you may have just lost your chance. From my time working in the field of graduate recruitment, it surprises me how many young people seem to mess the telephone interview up! We used to have over 1,000 people applying for jobs every week, and when we called them for their telephone interview we ended up rejecting over 75%. This is an enormous percentage and it could all have been so different if only they had followed these principles:

1. You must sound enthusiastic and **smile**. When a company calls you for a telephone interview, remember this is only the first step. You are facing tough competition, so sound like you're really pleased to hear from them! Strange as it may seem, a smile changes the tone of your voice and, even though you can't be seen, the interviewer will sense that you're smiling and will instantly warm to you. I would also encourage you to stand up, rather than sit down, as you will project your voice more and sound clearer.

2. **Listen** to their questions. Another common mistake young people make is that they don't hear the question because they haven't listened effectively enough. You must answer the question you have been asked. A good trick is to repeat the question once it is asked to you. For example, if asked, 'Why do you want to work for our company?' you would answer, 'I want to work for your company because...'

3. **Never** ask halfway through the call who the interviewer is and which company he is calling from! If you have listened effectively from the beginning, you would have taken in these details. I know that you have been applying to lots of different jobs and I'm sure the telephone interviewer does too, but remember everyone is human and humans are egocentric by nature. This means you must stroke the interviewer's ego and act as if this is the only company you have applied to and the only company you would ever want to work for. Don't worry – you'll find out these vital details later when they email you. Alternatively, a good trick is to take down an email address at the end and then you'll know.

4. Don't ramble or waffle – be concise in your answers! There is nothing more annoying to a telephone interviewer than a candidate who goes on and on about nothing. Listen to the question and then be concise in your answers by using the FEATURE, PROOF, BENEFIT rule. For example: 'Why do you want to work for our company?' 'I want to work for your company because *I have been doing lots of research on the sector* (FEATURE) and *I particularly like the new development in X space* (PROOF). *With this new thirst for knowledge and enthusiasm for this industry, I definitely feel I would be the best candidate for the job!'* (BENEFIT). The answer is short, concise and has a clear example and benefit statement. Try and answer all questions with this format.

5. **Close** for commitment – don't just let the interviewer hang up and say goodbye. Express your enthusiasm for the role and ask what the next steps are, and when you can expect an answer. Explain that you have been progressed to further interviews (even if you haven't)

with other companies, however this one is your favourite (stroking that ego).

If you follow all of these steps then I am certain you will be invited to the next step, which is often an assessment centre (see Chapter 5) or a face-to-face interview (see Chapter 6).

HOW TO USE SOCIAL MEDIA TO GET A JOB

LinkedIn is the world's largest professional network, with over 560 million members. It is the place where employers and recruiters are actively searching for people to hire, so it is really important that you build a strong profile on there. LinkedIn have even launched a new product called University Pages, aimed at helping graduates connect with peers and assisting you on building your careers by understanding and tracking how others have reached their career goals before you. They even suggest which university you should study at to reach your future goals.

To build the best profile possible you need to begin by thinking about what employers are looking for. Depending on your desired field and your natural skillset, the qualities you will want to highlight will be different. A project manager will want to highlight organisational, numerical and planning capabilities, while a salesperson will want to be perceived as a 'people person' with great negotiation and relationship-building skills.

Research what jobs are out there; speak to your parents and their friends about their career history and how they ended up doing what they are doing now. Start researching LinkedIn company pages and career pages to see what jobs are being recruited. Be aware that many industries are experiencing skills shortages and therefore demand in these areas will be strong. Some current examples include:

1. Nurses

2. Data analysts

3. Artificial intelligence/Robotics

4. Social workers

5. Software engineers

6. Mobile app developers and IOS developer roles (as a rough idea of the competition levels here, there are four or five for every company in London)

7. Anyone who delivers a service for a computer or an app

8. White collar construction talent

9. E-commerce skills – retailers are moving away from the high street and selling their clothes online. This means e-commerce and web development skills are very sought after

10. UX/UI designers

11. Digital marketing

12. Civil engineering and other types of engineering

13. Any white collar engineers

CREATING AN ONLINE PROFILE

When uploading a profile for a professional social media site such as LinkedIn, firstly you need to identify who you are and what your strengths are.

WHO ARE YOU?

In order to create the best online profile possible, you need to begin with the 'end in mind'. What are you trying to achieve with your profile? With the games tester example at the beginning of this book, I asked him to attach his new gaming blog to his profile and make it clear that he was passionate about working in gaming. If you still don't know what career direction you would like to take and are open to possibilities, use your profile to highlight your achievements and successes.

Another key point to remember is that LinkedIn's talent solutions business equates for the over 60% of their overall revenue. They have 50,000+ clients using this solution to find the best talent. One part of this solution is a direct sourcing tool that they are using to look for specific key words found in your profiles. You need to think about this when you are writing your profile. What keywords would recruiters be looking for? Use these within your qualifications, job titles, experience, etc. I would make it clear that you are a graduate looking to move into a certain sector or industry and then add lots of examples of where you have experienced success. The graduate recruitment officer of a company will search for specific 'grades', 'experience' and 'achievements'. You should include any groups or associations you participated in at university and also any work experience. You should also ask for recommendations, endorsements and referrals wherever possible.

ADD A PHOTO

The next step in building a successful online profile is including a professional image. I have seen numerous examples of terrible photos and whether we like it or not, people are making perceptions about us based on our appearance. Working at LinkedIn, I have seen way too many women with low cut tops and short skirts, and one man had even taken a selfie in a toilet and added it to his profile! Those images will certainly help you attract attention, but it will definitely be the wrong kind and you will end up in the reject pile. Please dress smartly and ensure the background is professional.

WRITE A PERSONALISED TAGLINE

Think of your tagline as your professional headline and brand, which will be used to grab the attention of a decision maker within the first three seconds.

The tagline I use is "Helping companies to find and attract the world's best talent via LinkedIn." It is short, concise and to the point, and tells people what I do very quickly. With the gaming tester example, he used "Passionate about everything to do with gaming, seeking a job in the gaming industry."

CREATE YOUR 'ELEVATOR' PITCH

Use the summary section to engage readers. Within five to ten seconds you need to:

- Capture their attention

- Showcase what you represent

- Sell yourself!

  The summary section is a place to tell an employer who you are, what you have done in the past and what you are interested in. For example within my LinkedIn profile

I explain that I am passionate about selling LinkedIn's talent solutions and tell the reader why. I also mention my background, which is running two successful recruitment companies and working for the fifth largest software company in the world in sales. I then explain about my passion and interest, which is coaching young people and graduates and that The Apprentice Project (www.theapprenticeproject.com) remains as an education resource for young people to help them find jobs.

Within this you can write who you are, what you studied and why, what you are looking to do in the future and the steps you have taken to get there. This is your chance to 'sell yourself' and explain why a company should hire you. You should write in the first person and detail your experience.

HIGHLIGHT YOUR SKILLS AND EXPERTISE

- Include the keywords recruiters are using to find you.

- Research what employers are looking for and add these skills to your profile if you possess them.

- Think like a recruiter! Search engine optimisation is very important in order to be found on LinkedIn. Optimise your profile with keywords related to the role that you want.

- Be honest with how you describe yourself.

GET RECOMMENDED BY PEOPLE YOU'VE HELPED

- Ask for meaningful recommendations

- Consider who you ask

- Request specifics, including context and details

- Ask people whom you genuinely believe you have helped.

If you truly have done a good job, then people will be more than happy to recommend you.

NOW IT'S TIME TO TAKE ACTION

- Complete your profile

- Ask relevant people for recommendations

- Start to build your external network

- Set a connection goal, for example 50 in the first month, then 100 in the first three months and 500+ after a year

- Link with friends, colleagues and people you meet

- Join relevant LinkedIn groups. For example if you want to move into engineering, join specific engineering groups on LinkedIn and start to connect with other like minded people on there

- Get involved in these groups. Start posting interesting and relevant content. Find articles and send them to people within the group

- Be disciplined. It takes time and focus to build a network and successfully meet people online, but the hard work will pay off!

ADDING SOCIAL MEDIA TO THE CV

It's a great idea to capitalise on your social media skills by featuring them in your CV Here are a few suggestions on how you could do this:

1. Start a blog and direct people to it, including a direct link on your CV and all social media profiles.

2. Start a Twitter account and write an effective subject line, such as 'Obsessed with everything to do with marketing ... looking to enter a growing company in a junior level marketing role'. Follow all the key players and companies in your chosen field and begin to network.

3. Use the same professional-looking photo for your profiles on LinkedIn, Twitter and all other social media accounts connected with your career.

4. Make sure your Facebook page is private and that personal photos of you letting your hair down on a Friday night cannot be accessed by anyone researching you on Google!

CHAPTER 5: ASSESSMENT CENTRES AND TESTING

An assessment centre, now what is that?

How do I behave? How do I act?

What will happen, what do I do?

All of this is very new.

How do they assess? How do I pass?

The answers are below, so just read and relax.

WHAT IS AN ASSESSMENT DAY?

An 'assessment day' is an important part of the recruitment process for many graduate employers. As the name suggests, it is a period of extended assessment that usually lasts for the best part of a day, and occasionally, two, or even three days.

Assessment days are extremely common, especially with graduate recruiters, as they are a great opportunity for employers to interview and screen many candidates at once. They are also a great opportunity for you to learn about them as an employer and what they can do for you and your career. I spent over six years running assessment centres on behalf of my clients including Accenture, Microsoft, Computer Associates, NTL, BT, Fujitsu, True Local, Yellow Pages, News Limited and

MySpace, and in this chapter I will let you know the secrets to successfully getting through!

Common sense...

Let's begin with a little common sense exercise so that we can enter the employer's mind. After reading this I want you to close your eyes, clear any other thoughts and really put yourself into the shoes of the employer running the assessment day. This employer wants to hire people for their organisation who are going to add value to their business. They will be paying hard-earned money to this individual, so it makes sense that they would be looking for someone who could provide them with a return on investment. What would a person look like who would add value? What would you see, hear and feel when you met a person like this? What competencies would this person possess? How would they act? Close your eyes and think about the answers to these questions, and then open your eyes and write down what comes to mind.

Now remember this person is **you**! You have been invited to the assessment day so that your future potential employer can screen you to see if you are that person that can add value to their business. I imagine the competencies you wrote down may look similar to these:

- Well-presented individual

- Good communication skills

- Ability to lead and work well in a team

- Ability to be independent and autonomous when required

- Thinks outside the box and brings creative ideas

- Displays analytical and problem-solving skills

- Is confident but not overbearing or arrogant

- Is driven and dynamic

- Demonstrates structured and logical thinking

- Has the ability to influence and persuade

- Asks intelligent questions and is interested in knowing more about the company

- Is really interested in working for this organisation

If you did come up with any of the above examples, then CONGRATULATIONS. Of course there will be plenty of other attributes that employers need depending on the individual role, for example you may have to display great mathematical skills or have achieved a certain grade, but in terms of generic personal competencies the above list is it.

So, how do you display these competencies and create a good impression?

I will take you through step-by-step in each area of an assessment day on how to behave and how to display these competencies.

RESEARCH

It is crucial that you research the company and complete the following questions prior to attending any assessment centre. Use LinkedIn, Twitter, Google, newspapers, journals, and competitors' websites for any relevant information, and ask any contacts you may have in the industry.

Make sure you can answer the following questions:

1. What does the company do?

2. Who are some of their competitors?

3. What's happening in their industry at the moment?

4. What competencies are they looking for in the role you have applied to?

5. How have I displayed any of those competencies at school, university or in previous work experience?

6. Why do I want to work for this company?

7. What are my strengths and what can I offer them as a business?

STEP 1

It is commonly known that people make up their minds about people in the first few seconds of meeting them. In fact Roger Ailes, the President of Fox News Channel believes, "You have just seven seconds to make a good first impression". Therefore **first impressions count**! In an assessment centre you will be required to register who you are before you sit down and this means meeting one of your judges right at the very beginning. Therefore:

• **Appearance counts** – be well presented! I have explored this further in Chapter 6, but it is vital that you look presentable. Girls must wear a dark suit, a white blouse, little to no jewellery and very natural make-up. No liquid eyeliner or odd piercings allowed. Wear your hair neatly and carry a smart looking handbag that matches your suit. Please wear closed toe black shoes. I know this may sound boring but believe me, you want to create a professional image, and this is how to do so. Boys must also wear a dark suit, polish their shoes and have dark socks. Remove any piercings and wear no jewellery (apart from perhaps a respectable watch). Please take a smart man bag or briefcase and don't wear sunglasses. Everyone should walk tall when approaching the registering station.

- **It's all in the handshake**. A lot of people don't realise how important a strong, firm shake can be! Through a handshake you can tell a lot about a person. Shake hands with confidence and smile; be firm but not aggressive. Start by practicing on friends and family. Even women appreciate a strong handshake so don't be afraid! However, make sure to judge the situation and don't hurt anyone...

- **Make eye contact** when shaking hands.

- **Project energy and passion**. This is the time to stand out from the other 20 candidates.

- I would also suggest rehearsing sounding smart by putting together a couple of intelligent sentences. Being articulate is more valuable to me than your degree.

STEP 2

Often an assessment day will begin with a presentation by the employer about what they do and what they can offer you as a candidate. Even when the presentation is on and you're not required to talk, **you are being judged**. Make sure you are listening attentively and think of intelligent questions to ask. You can reserve these for the interview later as it shows you were listening, however it may also be appropriate to ask sooner if they offer some space to ask questions.

The self-introduction session

This is your chance to let the audience know who you are and how you can demonstrate value. Take some deep breaths to calm any nerves (again, I would recommend practicing at home before you even go to the assessment centre). Avoid trying to be the class clown and make sure your self-introduction is business-minded and/or achievements-based, and demonstrates how you can offer value to their organisation. I would stand up, be confident and give eye contact to everyone in the room but mainly at the JUDGES. Speak to them – all of them – giving the same amount of eye contact to each. This helps you personalise yourself, and each judge will remember you individually and will score you highly. Remember the competencies you are being judged for and highlight that you display all of them.

STEP 3 – Group exercises

This is the part of the day when you are split into teams and asked to work as a group. There are a number of things the employer is looking for and it's not necessarily the loudest voice! A group exercise is not a competition. Employers will be looking for you to be friendly, polite and supportive to other candidates. Assessors are looking for competitive people who can work well with others, not just competitive people. Teamwork is the key.

The most important thing is to get involved but get involved *intelligently*. Work your way to the inner circle of the group and make some thoughtful suggestions. Listen to the other people and even tell them, 'Well done' or say, 'That's a great point!' This demonstrates your leadership skills and ability to work well in a team. It will also encourage the group to work with you and look up to you because they will subconsciously begin to seek your praise. You don't have to have the loudest voice but you do need to be heard. Perhaps grab the pen or read the exercise to the group and let them know that you're part of the group and there to be listened to.

PSYCHOMETRIC TESTING

A lot of graduates seem to be scared of psychometric and personality testing, however the good news on a personality test is there are no right or wrong answers. The purpose is to find out who you are and which style of management would best suit you.

Employers also want to know if you are a good match for their company and this will only benefit you too.

Common FAQs

Q: Will psychometric tests happen in a big hall or a small cubicle?

A: Most of the time you will be sent the psychometric test to complete online within your own time.

Q: Will they take place on a computer or on paper?

A: Psychometrics tests usually take place on the computer.

Q: Will other people be able to see my answers?

A: No – your answers will be scored immediately by the computer's algorithms.

Q: What if my answers are wrong or I can't think of an answer to give?

A: There are no wrong answers in psychometric personality tests. If you don't know the answer, guess.

Q: Will I find out my results on the day?

A: This depends entirely on the company, but you can always ask in advance if you are curious.

Competency-based interviews

I will address interviews at length in the following chapter, but competency-based interviews are the preferred style of interview during an assessment day, as they are the best way to uncover behavioural aspects of an individual in a quick and precise manner.

They uncover the following things:

A. Your initiative to solve problems

B. Your achievements

C. The most difficult incident you have had to handle and how you did so

D. Your leadership skills

Before attending the assessment day I would recommend writing the answers down to the following questions. Think of examples drawn from school, university or even from previous work experiences.

1. **When have you had to solve a problem?**
What was the problem? What steps did you take to handle it? What did you learn from this? Was there a positive or negative outcome and how might this benefit a future employer?

2. **What is your greatest achievement?**
What is it? Why would you describe this as an 'achievement'? What did you learn from this? What skills did it give you and how would they benefit a future employer?

3. **What are your weaknesses?**
There are two schools of thought when it comes to answering this question, so please go with your gut. Some people suggest mentioning a weakness that could also be considered a positive. For example:

"I find it hard to delegate my work and often take control of all of it when it would be wiser to delegate some of it."

"I'm a classic overachiever which means I often take on too much work and then I wear myself down, when really if I had taken smaller, more manageable steps, I could be more productive."

"I'm slightly egocentric," said with a smile, "meaning I think I'm good because I've had a lot of achievements in my life [*give examples*]. However I also know it is much better to be modest and humble, and that is something I am working on."

"I beat myself up when I don't know something. I love to learn and have a constant desire to improve myself. This can be considered a weakness, as I never give myself praise or credit for what I do know already."

If you don't feel any of the above answers are authentic for you, a great piece of advice is to remain honest. First, spend some time thinking about what your weaknesses actually are. Then, in the interview, discuss your weaknesses in terms of how you've managed to conquer them or turn them into strengths during your experiences. Alan Cutter, CEO of AC Lion, a leading recruitment company in New York says that you need to make sure to tread the fine line between confidence and conceit, as well as the line between vulnerability and incompetency. During your competency-based interview, bear in mind the following tips, which will be further explored in Chapter 6:

- Be clear, concise and to the point

- Listen effectively – you would be surprised the amount of people who don't even hear the question they been asked and start answering something completely random! This is a big no-no. Effective listening is vital.

- Use the FEATURE, PROOF, BENEFIT rule. Always back up everything you say with an example of where you have demonstrated it before and discuss how it can benefit the employer.

- Ask a couple of intelligent questions at the end of the interview, which demonstrates your interest in the role and their company. Talk about something that is happening in the industry. Let them know that you have put thought into this interview and that you want the job.

- Always be professional when answering. This means don't be negative about any of your past experiences. If you had a difficult situation, talk about it professionally and never bad-mouth or be rude about anyone.

- Close for commitment. Always end the interview by demonstrating your enthusiasm for the role. Explain that this is your first choice company and that you really want to work there. Ask your interviewers what the next steps will be and when you will hear from them. This part is crucial to your success!

Practice makes perfect

If you're lucky enough to be invited to many assessment days even with companies you wouldn't consider working for, I encourage you to go anyway. Firstly, you don't know what a company has to offer unless you go and you may be surprised. Secondly, and more importantly, it gives you an opportunity to practice your assessment day skills, so you are better prepared for when you finally attend an assessment day held by your dream employer.

Remember: everything happens for a reason, so if you're unsuccessful, then it was probably in your best interests. Something better will be around the corner!

CHAPTER 6: ALL ABOUT INTERVIEWS

An interview can be lots of fun,

It's the final hurdle before a job can be won.

Do you like them? Do they like you?

Go be yourself, but that's not all you should do.

There are hints and tricks and ways to prepare,

So read this chapter and you'll almost be there!

There is so much information available about how to be the best you can be in a job interview. Much of this concentrates on researching the company and making yourself come across as well as possible, however what is missing is that there is a certain 'human' element to interviews. You are being questioned and judged by a person, and it is useful to remember that that person will have already made up his or her mind about whether to interview you within the first few seconds of viewing your CV He or she will have decided if you are smart, capable and employable even before you open your mouth.

So what are the factors influencing these decisions and how can you use them to your advantage to ensure you get the job?

As a Master NLP practitioner, I have studied where beliefs are formed and how they enter our subconscious mind. Once you understand that 96% of what we do, think and feel is subconscious, it enables us to start challenging our belief systems and potentially change them.

We make subconscious perceptions about people all the time. We judge people on the way they dress, talk, eat and walk, and this can be positive or negative. We decide if someone is worthy of our time pretty quickly and the same is true in an interview situation. There are, of course, certain attributes that all employers look for, including a demonstrated passion for the role, a high level of confidence that you will be able to do the role, and tenacity and enthusiasm.

The good news is most of these traits are 'perceived'. If you *act* confident externally, then people will believe that you *are* confident. As confidence has such a positive effect on people, this is an incredibly important skill. People will perceive you to be more capable and reliable. They will warm to you and trust you. They will believe you will complete everything you say you will and in a job interview, they will want to hire you!

So how do you improve your confidence? The trick is to 'model excellence', i.e. think of people whom you consider to be confident. How do they walk? How do they carry themselves? How do they sit and stand? How do they talk? What you'll find is that confident people walk with their heads held high, their shoulders back and have a relaxed face. They won't waffle and will get to the point quickly and easily. They will be immaculately presented and will listen attentively to everything they are asked before responding.

It is important to keep this in mind prior to your job interview and ensure you get yourself into this confident state. Other top tips are:

Dress the part
I'll discuss appearance in more depth later in this chapter, but for

now, when it comes to a job interview, you will find that 'people like people like themselves'. You only have to look around at most companies to see that they hire similar people. I would take note of employees' dress and what kind of personalities come through on their social media profiles. Are they a serious company? Cool? Creative? Professional? You want to ensure you 'fit in' with their culture and dress accordingly. If in doubt, always look smart and professional, with minimal jewellery.

Be interested and interesting

It is vitally important to show an interest in the person who is interviewing you and also have entertaining stories to share about yourself. An interviewer wants to see that you have leisure pursuits outside of work and that you can bring additional value to the team.

Put yourself in their shoes

Try to put yourself into the mindset of the people interviewing you. The best way to do this is to utilise social media. Do they have LinkedIn profiles? What is their background? If someone has written an article before, positively comment on it. If they have worked at the company many years, ask them about how they have found certain changes. It is also important to know what is happening in the industry and what the company's growth plans are. You can read news articles about the company and Google them for further insights.

Ask intelligent questions

Interviewers are looking for someone to be interested in their industry and what is happening with the company. They are also looking for someone who will add value to their business and fit in with the culture of the company. See later in this chapter for examples of great questions to ask at the end of the interview.

Be passionate about their industry and the role

The number one trait employers look for when they interview candidates is finding someone who is passionate about their industry. Passion and enthusiasm are infectious.

Be specific

Answer questions with examples of how you have demonstrated certain competencies. Don't just say you have leadership skills. Use specific examples of when you have demonstrated these skills and then discuss the benefit of your skill to their business.

'Close them down'

You should always display your enthusiasm and passion for the role before the interview ends, by asking them what the next steps are. The interviewer needs to know that you want the job and are determined to get it.

DELVING DEEPER

Firstly it is important to try to understand why a role would have become available in the first place. I suggest you close your eyes and imagine the boardroom meeting that would have occurred prior to the role being advertised. What had happened beforehand? Did someone leave? Is the company expanding? What is important about this particular role?

Once you are in that frame of mind, it's time to turn your attention to what is important to the company you are interviewing with. What is their mission statement?

Consciously and subconsciously, every single interview question you will ever be asked, every reason you will be screened out and hired, and every reason you could get fired or promoted comes from the company's definition of what is important to them. I met the PR team of a very famous fashion label recently and everyone there was pretty, slim and brunette. Somewhere in the subconscious minds of the hiring process, they were looking to hire pretty clones to represent their brand effectively.

Whether you like it or not, as soon as you are hired into a company you are a representation of the brand and therefore matching values, goals and mission statement is crucial.

For example, if the company prides itself on an attitude of great customer service, then you should focus on this in your CV and in your interview, demonstrating when and how you have delivered great customer service. If part of the company's motivation is 'giving back to the community', then start volunteering and highlight this on your CV To succeed you may need to adjust how you talk, dress or act during your job search purely to match what is expected in the new company culture.

Presentation is crucial and this is not just about looking good. It is about looking, sounding and acting like the employer. That famous fashion label I was referring to above is a perfect example as to why all their staff look and dress similarly. They want everyone to positively represent the company to the public and co-workers. So you will be scrutinised on everything from your clothing and hairstyle to your handshake and hygiene, from your accent and grammar to your eye contact and body language, and from the type of work you have done in the past to your current accomplishments and achievements.

Remember, one common question employers ask themselves when they interview you is, "Do you look, sound and act in a way that positively represents my company?"

THE FIRST TEN SECONDS MATTER

"The first 10% of any interview will dictate the final 90%"

As I have already mentioned, you are being interviewed by a 'person' and there is a human element to all interviews. We have all heard the phrase, "people make up their mind about you in the first few seconds of meeting you" and this is certainly true for employers and interviewers.

So what happens in those first few seconds? How do these quick opinions get formed? How do the employers decide if you are a 'yes' or a 'no' almost immediately?

As I mentioned earlier, 96% of what we do, think and feel is subconscious and that creates our beliefs, opinions, values and perceptions. This means that, without us really knowing it, our subconscious is forming opinions of people all the time, which allows us to make quick judgements. Within just ten seconds, we decide who is confident, smart, successful and employable before they even open their mouth! This is an important fact to know when going on job interviews, because it's possible to create an amazing first impression almost immediately.

The best way to do this is to really think about what characteristics you might see in people that would enable you to perceive them as confident, smart, successful and employable. What would they look like? What clothes are these confident people wearing? How are they standing? What questions do they ask? How do they speak? Can you think of any famous people who emulate confidence? What is it about them that has caused you to formulate your positive opinion and perception of them?

This exercise forms the basis for some key tips on first impressions:

- Firstly, punctuality is vital! You must never be LATE for an interview. If you are unsure of the journey or how long it will take, you must plan the route the day before. I would advise to practise the relevant public transport route or the drive there to ensure you know exactly where you are going. You can never build strong rapport when you have arrived late. Equally it is important not to arrive too early. Your interviewer has set a specific time aside and as they are very busy individuals they won't want to rush their tasks just because you are waiting in reception. I recommend arriving five to ten minutes before.

- Secondly, always be standing waiting in reception for your interviewer. If you are already standing it suggests that you are ready, prepared and confident! It will make you stand out from other candidates who may have been slouched in the chair, reading a magazine.

- Look smart and presentable. Wear smart clothes, minimal jewellery and polish your shoes – and read my section on 'Appearance' below!

- Build rapport on topics the person will be interested in, using your online research to your benefit. Mirror their behaviour; ask them about their background and about themselves. I would encourage you to read *How To Win Friends And Influence People* by Dale Carnegie.

- Send an email after the interview, thanking your interviewers for their time.

APPEARANCE

So let me get this straight. You don't have to be Kate Moss or Brad Pitt to get a job but personal appearance does go a long way! As we've already discussed, it has been scientifically proven that people make up their minds about you in the first few seconds of meeting you, so what you look like is a big part of this first impression.

For an interview I would recommend that girls wear a smart suit with a shirt (ironed of course), please wear clear, tanned tights (even if it is hot outside) and polished, closed toe black shoes. I know this sounds boring, but it is so important to look smart! If you were going for more of a creative role I advise to wear a coloured shirt or top but still stick to the black skirt, tights and closed toe shoes rule.

Girls' hair should be washed and styled in a professional manner. Either tie it back or wear it very smart. Jewellery should be minimal and tasteful. When it comes to make-up, again, minimal is key, but please ensure you have a little eye makeup on, to show that you have made an effort. Steer clear from bright eye shadows, bright lipsticks or liquid eyeliner!

For boys, as I have previously mentioned you should be clean-shaven and wear a smart suit. If you are interviewing with a financial services company, you should wear a tie. If you are interviewing with an Internet company, you won't need to wear a tie. Please use your judgment, but remember smarter is better.

You should remove all piercings, hide any tattoos and remain as professional as possible.

BODY LANGUAGE

One of the best techniques to building rapport is all about 'mirroring' behaviour. It makes sense that if your interviewer is sat back in his or her chair and you are crouched forward, there may be some awkwardness!

It may sound strange, but research shows that imitating other people's nonverbal expressions can help you understand the emotions they are experiencing. Since we all express our emotions nonverbally, copying those expressions affects our own emotions due to an "afferent feedback mechanism." In short: mimic my expressions and you'll better understand how I feel – which means you can better help me work through those feelings. Plus, mimicking facial expressions (something we do often without thinking) makes the other person feel the interaction was more positive.

When your interviewers greet you, smile and shake hands with a strong, firm grip (I recommend practicing with a friend or family member beforehand). Gesture to yourself when saying your name and comment that it is, "Lovely to meet them." When offered water or any other drink always say, 'Yes please,' as this puts you in a position of power and demonstrates that you are confident.

When the interview begins, please watch how your interviewers sit in their chair. If they are sat back, you *must* sit back. If they are leaning forward, you *must* lean forward. I understand this is often difficult when you are nervous but if you purposefully mirror body language at the beginning, soon it will become natural and you will make your interviewer feel comfortable around you.

An interview should flow like a conversation with a friend, but with much less colloquialism! Your language should be professional and you should listen intently to every question. Take note of their style. Are they pragmatic, i.e. do they get to the point quickly? Are they expressive? Do they smile and use stories? Are they detail orientated? Do they use facts and figures and statistics? Or are they amiable? This will be important in determining how to answer your questions and in which style.

For example, if your interview is with a very direct, fast-paced individual (and in most cases it will be) and you take your time answering your question, you run the risk of annoying them! Your interviewer will be getting agitated, as he or she will want you to 'hurry up'. You must therefore answer your questions quickly and concisely. However, if your interviewer is expressive, you can smile and tell a story, as this will help you to build rapport. If your interviewer is detail-orientated, then use lots of examples, times, dates and figures etc.

According to Harvard professor Amy Cuddy's famous TED talk, two minutes of power posing – standing tall, holding your arms out or towards the sky, or standing like Superman with your hands on your hips – will dramatically increase your level of confidence. Try this one before stepping into an interview or an assessment centre. I advise to hide somewhere and get into these power poses and see how confident you feel! Trust me: it works. Other tips include:

Smile

Mark Bowden, body language expert, suggests that smiling, or even forcing yourself to smile will trick your brain into thinking that you are relaxed and happy. Frowning, grimacing, and other negative facial expressions signal to your brain that whatever you are doing is difficult. When you make yourself smile, you will feel less stressed, even if nothing else about the situation changes.

Talk with your hands to improve clarity

Think about how you talk and act when you're comfortable. Say you're telling a story at a party. You use your hands naturally and the right gestures add immeasurably to your words. Act the same way when you're in an interview. Using your hands when you speak will help you feel more confident, think more clearly, more naturally punctuate certain words and phrases, and fall into a much better rhythm. Loosen up and don't think about your hands. Just let them go. The impact on your words will be dramatic.

Use eye contact

Eye contact implies confidence, honesty and openness. Also try flashing your eyebrows just occasionally – this signals that I recognise you and you are my friend.

THE THREE BEST INTERVIEW QUESTIONS TO ASK

You've made it through to an interview and now is your time to shine! Following are my top three questions to ask at the end of the interview, but firstly you need to remember the two key things most employers think about when recruiting are:

1. Will this person help me make money?

2. Will they get on with the team?

The most common reasons people get fired in their probation period are that they fail to demonstrate how they can add value (save time, make money, etc.) or they simply don't fit in with the culture of the organisation.

Therefore the three best interview questions to ask are as follows:

1. What is the culture of the company like? Do you see me fitting in?

This question demonstrates that you know how important cultural fit is and that you are not scared to find out if it is the right company for you, and vice versa.

2. In your opinion, what competencies make people really successful in this role?

Once you have listened to the information you can then start thinking and reiterating examples of where you have demonstrated those competencies. Start the sentence by saying, "I am really glad you mentioned those things, as that is where I see my strengths lying. For example, I once had to do X, Y and Z [*relate this to the competencies mentioned*] and I can see those skills being valuable in this role too."

3. What is your background? And what are your favourite things about this company?

This suggests you are interested in the person who is interviewing you. As everyone likes to feel important and have his or her ego stroked, this is a brilliant question to ask. You are also expressing a keen interest in working for the company and want to know why they took a job there.

Other intelligent questions examples are as follows:

I hope I've hammered in by now the importance of research, research, research! And please don't just look at the website. Start looking at industry trends, read the news, read trade publications and sign up for Google Alerts. This research will have a direct impact on the type of questions you should ask at interview.

IT

If you were going for an interview for an IT company and you notice that all organisations are moving to a software as a service model, you could ask what is their strategy as a business for keeping ahead of this new trend and shift in IT thinking? Similarly, how has the hype of 'Artificial Intelligence', 'cloud computing' and 'virtualisation' shifted the strategy for their business?

Fashion

How have the new designs and colours we are seeing at today's fashion shows affected your strategy as a business and fashion house? Who are your leading designer inspirations?

Media

How has the rise of 'fake news' impacted their business? What are their steps for digital transformation and how is that affecting their business?

If you can ask intelligent questions focused on the latest news in a particular industry, then you will come across well.

HOW TO FOLLOW UP AFTER AN INTERVIEW

James Caan recently wrote a great article about the importance of following up after an interview and I couldn't agree more.

Lots of employers I speak to think really highly about this as it ensures you stand out from the crowd and that they remember you. It is also a great opportunity to express your passion and enthusiasm for the role and that you enjoyed meeting that person.

James writes that as soon as you finish the interview, you should take down notes – it's all too easy to forget key things that may have happened. Jot down what you think went well, what you feel you should have covered more – and most importantly, any useful nugget of information you may have picked up about the role or company.

You will be able to find out their email address really easily by just calling up and asking for it after explaining that you want to follow up. You can also find them on LinkedIn where you can connect and send an inmail. Keep the follow up email short and to the point: no more than five or six lines.

You should start by thanking them for their time. Then you can discuss a specific point they may have mentioned. This could be about their growth plans, an acquisition they are going through, new products being launched etc. Whatever it is, by briefly touching upon it you are demonstrating great listening skills and genuine interest.

James Caan then speaks about the most important part of a follow-up email, which is the place where you 'sell yourself' as someone who is passionate and excited about the role. Say something along the lines of, "I'm really excited about the opportunity you are offering; this seems like an exciting time for the business and the role is a great fit for my skillset and experience. If you need any additional documents or information from me, do let me know."

This is all you need. You've demonstrated your passion, enthusiasm and interest for the role, and you have politely thanked them for their time and explained that you enjoyed meeting them. If you haven't heard back after a couple of weeks, then you are perfectly entitled to follow up. You should remain polite at all times and ask for an updated timeframe. You can do this by phone or email.

THE MOST COMMON MISTAKES GRADUATES MAKE IN AN INTERVIEW

Based on my eight years of working in the field of graduate recruitment, I have written below the Top Six most common mistakes graduates make at an interview and what you can do to improve your chances of securing a job.

1. Failing to do enough preparation for the interview

There's no excuse. You need to know as much information as possible about the company (what do they do? Who started it? When was it started?). You need to know their competitors by name and some reasons why the company you are interviewing with is better. You need to be informed on any new developments within the industry – think about how this company can grow their business and what ideas you have to facilitate this growth. Also, don't just research the company; research the people interviewing you. Who are they? What personality types do you suspect they have? What roles do they perform? What might be important to them? Have you read their Twitter feed? Their blog? Their LinkedIn profile?

2. Not demonstrating a clear passion or focus that you want this role

The number one thing employers are looking for is a passion for the role. If the CV hasn't been tailored specifically according to the role or there has been no clear effort to study or learn more about their industry, then you will immediately be caught out.

3. Having no intelligent questions to ask at the end

Surely if you were about to devote a large amount of time to a company and a role, then you would have questions to ask? Employers see questions as a demonstrable enthusiasm to work for their company.

4. Having no examples to back up where you can add value

It is important to know how you can add value to a company. Look back at previous experience, public speaking history, participation in the Duke of Edinburgh's Award programme or Young Enterprise, playing sport or music at school, acting in a school play, holding down a paper round, or being part of a society at university. Now think about what competencies you have developed, which can add value to an employer. Did the experience improve your communication skills, meaning you can liaise with clients with ease? Did it improve your leadership skills? What about your confidence?

5. Graduates not knowing what they want to do
In an interview the employer is looking for evidence that the person they are interviewing wants the job, I mean *really* wants the job, and whether or not they have the ability to do the job. If the candidate umms and ahhs about why they want to work there, then this will immediately put the employer off. An employer only wants to see a demonstrated and proven enthusiasm for the role and for working at their company with valid reasons why.

6. They don't appear warm or friendly enough at the interview stage
Due to all the nerves of an interview situation, most graduates forget the most important criteria, which is that people like to be surrounded by positive energy and positive people. The interview should centre on building rapport and showing how you would fit into the team. A little research on the person interviewing you using social media can give you lots of ideas to help you build rapport and be less nervous.

"In an interview the employer is looking for evidence that the person they are interviewing wants the job, I mean really wants the job, and whether or not they have the ability to do the job."

Finally, here are some hints and tips for addressing common employer complaints and mistakes made in interviews:

1. Make it your business to fully understand about the role, what is expected from you and have some good reasons why you are passionate and focused about this area.

2. Turn off your mobile phone and iPod.

3. Don't smell of alcohol or cigarettes, use deodorant and have a mint to freshen your breath before you go in.

4. Don't interrupt or contradict the interviewer.

5. Never swear – even if the employer does. This is one behaviour you don't want to mirror!

6. Avoid fidgeting – it's irritating and makes you appear nervous.

7. Thank the interviewer for their time afterwards – sending a follow-up email is also a great idea.

CHAPTER 7: HOW TO BECOME MORE EMOTIONALLY INTELLIGENT

"When you know better, you do better."
Maya Angelou

Have you ever found yourself in a situation where you have met somebody and after talking together for two minutes, you felt like you have been friends forever? Or alternatively, have you ever been in a situation where no matter how hard you tried, you just couldn't get the person you were speaking with to like you?

Understanding why this happens is crucial to realising how you can become more **emotionally intelligent**. Emotional intelligence is a vital skill to learn as it allows you to see from the other person's perspective and enables you to connect with everybody.

As a qualified iMA Practitioner, I would like to introduce you to the following website:

http://ima-connecting.com

Here the 'i' stands for identify your iMA colour style and that of the person you want to connect with. The 'M' stands for Modify your message by encoding in a way that is most likely to be understood. Finally, the 'A' stands for Adapt the way you treat one person over another. On this website I would like you to fill out the quick iMA personality questionnaire to determine your personality style. (This information will be kept confidential; your data will not be used). After just a minute or so, you will be assigned a colour based on your responses and you will be ready to learn how you can communicate with people with different styles to you. Once you begin to understand more about yourself and your natural style, you will discover what needs to be adapted in an interview situation to make the interviewer feel comfortable and at ease. This will enhance your chances of landing your dream job significantly.

After completing the questionnaire and noting your colour, please read on to find out how you can start understanding different personality types, change your own self-limiting beliefs and build a rapport with everyone.

EXPLAINING IMA

We are living in exciting, challenging, turbulent times. Every graduate is looking for that elusive competitive edge. Your effectiveness, success, happiness and future are dependent on your ability to connect with others.

When you connect with someone they see the best in you, meaning:

- They give you their time and attention

- They place weight on what you say

- They make allowances for your shortcomings

- They focus on your strengths

- They are willing to assist you

- They make themselves available and do not avoid you

With the above in mind, your ability to connect with others directly determines your quality of life.

Connectivity is a fundamental life skill and up until now little or no training has been available. iMA teaches you the things you need to know or be reminded of to connect with anyone at any level of your life.

Everyone in the world speaks one of four possible iMA dialects, putting him or her on the same wavelength as 25% of the people in the global population. This also means that everyone is in the minority and that 75% of people have different traits, perspectives, opinions and approaches.

Of those 75%, many will be important to your success, both in and out of the workplace. These people

- Think differently

- Decide differently

- Work at a different pace

- Use time differently

- Communicate differently

- Handle emotions differently

- Manage stress differently

- Deal with conflicting opinions differently

There are clearly many problems associated with being so different! When people are different from one another, they

- Have a harder time connecting

- Miscommunicate more often

- Are less likely to influence others

- Are less likeable than others

- Rub each other the wrong way, just by being themselves

The universal language of iMA is a simple way of observing and understanding the differences in people, and connecting with others on their wavelength.

When this happens, communication, trust, understanding, co-operation and sales go up, and stress and tension levels go down.

HOW TO IDENTIFY DIFFERENT IMA DIALECTS

People differ in many ways, from their appearance and beliefs to their mannerisms, value and much, much more. To understand how to connect with people, first you need to identify two elements of observable behaviour.

The first element is to determine whether a person is **Right Brain Thinking** or **Left Brain Thinking**.

Right Brain Thinking people
Right Brain Thinking people are ready and willing to:

- Enter into and initiate relationships

- Share and show their thoughts and feelings

- Accept others when they share and show their thoughts and feelings

- Be relaxed and warm

- Wear their heart on their sleeves

- Focus on the needs of people

- Make decisions based on intuition

- Go with the flow rather than stick to schedules

- Be flexible on how their time is used by others

- Have flexible expectations about people and situations

- Initiate and/or accept physical contact

- Display animated facial expressions, hand and body movement

- Express their opinions readily

- Be easy to get to know in business and social situations

People give out plenty of clues if they are Right Brain Thinking. Listen to what they say and watch what they do, as it can be quite obvious. **Verbal clues** involve telling stories or anecdotes, sharing personal feelings, using informal speech and expressing opinions readily. **Vocal clues** include using lots of inflection, and more variation in pitch and vocal quality. There will also be plenty of **visual clues**, such as making frequent eye contact, constantly changing facial expressions, spontaneous use of hands and physical gestures, being contact-oriented, relaxed and dramatic.

Left Brain Thinking People
By contrast, Left Brain Thinking people are not nearly as open and are characterised by being self-contained. These people

- Don't readily share and show their feelings

- Take longer to 'warm up' in conversation

- Like to keep a mental and physical distance

- Make decisions based on logic

- Are fact and task-oriented

- Exhibit limited sharing of personal feelings

- Use more formal speech

- Reserve expression of opinions

- Prefer to follow established schedules

- Focus conversation and stay on the subject

- Avoid or minimise physical contact

- Prefer to work independently

- Take time to get to know others in unfamiliar business and social situations

- Are disciplined on how time is used by others

- Are more likely to be expressionless during speaking

- Tend to have fixed expectations about people and situations

Again, there are many clues to pick up on with Left Brain Thinking people. **Verbal clues** include being fact and task-oriented, preferring not to talk about themselves and not giving opinions.

Vocal clues are speech with little inflection, fewer pitch variations and less variety in vocal qualities. Finally, **visual clues** are suggested by fewer facial expressions, showing a controlled or limited hand and body movement, being non-contact oriented, being generally guarded and slow in giving non-verbal feedback.

The second element of observable behaviour is **Assertiveness**.

Assertiveness can be typified by a person's need to move forward, the way a person deals with information and the situation, and the degree of forcefulness that person uses in expressing his or her thoughts, feeling and emotions.

Assertive People

- Tend to be impatient and move at a quick pace

- Are outspoken, dominant, talkative and extrovert

- Approach risk change easily and make decisions quickly

- Are frequent contributors to group conversations

- Frequently use gestures, voice intonation to emphasise points

- Often makes emphatic statements like, "This is so..." and "I'm positive that..."

- Express opinions readily

- Are less patient and more competitive

- Can be confronting and controlling

- Are more likely to maintain their positions during disagreements

- Sustain eye contact

- Are more likely to introduce themselves at social gatherings, and give firm handshakes

- Tend to bend or break established rules and policies

As with Left and Right Brain Thinking people, assertive people provide a number of clues as to their type. **Verbal clues** include being talkative, opinionated and emphatic. **Vocal clues** encompass using faster speech patterns, and talking more forcefully at a high volume. Finally, clear **visual clues** include steady eye contact, a firm handshake, and gesticulation such as pointing and impatience.

Non-Assertive people

- Move at a slower pace

- Approach risk, change and decisions slowly and deliberately

- Are compliant, patient and co-operative

- Are supportive

- Tend to ask or speak more tentatively, and are softly spoken

- Take a roundabout approach, or go slowly

- Are infrequent contributors to group discussions

- Employ only infrequent use of gestures and voice intonation to emphasise points

- Reserve expression of opinion

- Are diplomatic and collaborative

- Are understated and reserved

- Only maintain intermittent eye contact

- Are more likely to wait for others to introduce themselves at social gatherings

- Have a gentle handshake

- Tend to follow established rules and policies

Verbal clues that a person is non-assertive include listening, reserving opinion, only asking questions for clarification and making qualified statements. **Vocal clues** betraying such a personality type might be a steady even delivery, being less forceful, communicating slower and more sparingly and at a lower volume. Finally, **visual clues** might be a gentle handshake, intermittent eye contact, limited physical gestures and patience.

With four patterned and predictable behaviour styles and two elements to consider, there are four possible personality combinations as follows:

Right Brain + Non-Assertive	= **High Blue**
Left Brain + Non-Assertive	= **High Green**
Left Brain + Assertive	= **High Red**
Right Brain + Assertive	= **High Yellow**

If you haven't already done so, why don't you complete the brief online personality test at http://ima-connecting.com to confirm what you are – are your suspicions correct? For a more detailed breakdown of the iMA colours and personality types, please see Appendix 1.

Remember: the key to success is **adaptability**. Once you understand the key principles of iMA, then you will be more

- Confident

- Tolerant

- Positive

- Empathetic

- Respectful (by understanding, accepting and appreciating the differences)

"If you can make a person like themselves better… They will love you!"
iMA philosophy

THE HIDDEN JOB MARKET

"Thinking like everyone else will keep you unemployed"

In poor economic times fewer employers advertise their jobs partly due to a lack of funds and partly because of the inevitable influx of applications. I had one client who, prior to hiring my recruitment services, posted a newspaper advert and received over 600 applications. My client had neither the staff nor the resources to check or follow up the applications and therefore it was an entirely wasted exercise.

With this in mind it becomes obvious that the traditional way of applying for jobs by answering an advert has become redundant. During my time working at LinkedIn, I can confidently say that talent acquisition has changed and companies are moving to a direct sourcing model. They are stopping using agencies and they are sourcing the best talent themselves. They are using LinkedIn to directly headhunt applicants themselves and this is great news for you. Most of your talent competition are still heavily reliant on using agencies to find a job for them, however if the companies are no longer using agencies as much, this provides a great opportunity for you! You need to start moving through the 'side door' and this is where networking and having a passion and a focus become very important.

Employers often have a 'refer a friend' system in house and encourage their employees to refer people who might be good for their company. So the best idea for you is to identify the companies you would want to work for. Using LinkedIn, start to list everyone you know, socially and professionally, who could potentially introduce you to the decision-makers at these companies.

You can also access the hidden market by **proactively contacting employers directly**. The rise of social media sites such as Twitter and LinkedIn have made this relatively easy to do. Most employers put off advertising new positions as long as they can due to the cost and time involved, so making contact is an excellent idea.

After choosing the company you want to target, aim at it with passion, enthusiasm and energy. When you find the right person to write to, try the sample text outlined in Appendix 2 as the basis of an introductory letter. If you don't get a response (whether positive or negative) after a month, contact them once again to check to see if they received your letter. Send them a copy and say you'd really appreciate at least a formal or informal interview.

I know this may seem a scary and daunting prospect, especially as a graduate with no experience, but it proves that you have the proactive attitude and determination to succeed, and this is exactly what employers are looking for. Just like people, companies have egos too, and what could be more flattering than someone who only wants to work for them and has the courage to directly approach them to say as much? Not only do you have nothing to lose, but it's also a guaranteed strategy to make you stand you out from the crowd. This was the path I recommended to the career-coaching candidate I first mentioned in the introduction to this book. After contacting employers directly, he secured his dream job at SEGA as a games tester. This would never have happened had he applied through traditional methods just like everyone else.

Familiarity feels safe and after a long time in the recruitment world I have learnt how debilitating self-doubt and fear can be. You feel that the easiest thing is to give up – especially if you watch the news and hear the stories of how 'impossible' it is to get a job and the latest youth unemployment figures. The truth is, fear among jobseekers is the norm. You wonder if you have any value to add and believe that no one will hire you. The following techniques may help you conquer fear along the way.

Conquer the fear exercise

1. Write down two things that you are really good at. It could be playing a musical instrument, computer skills, playing sports, acting, writing, singing, looking after your little brother, coming up with business ideas, playing video games, organising events, etc.

2. Now write down three reasons why each of those skills is valuable. For example, playing a musical instrument means that you are open to learning, you are committed and dedicated, and you have the attitude of regular practice.

3. Think about what would happen if you were proactive and applied for a job directly. What is the worst that could happen? How would that make you feel? Would it *really* be the end of the world?

4. Think about a time when you were particularly nervous about an event. It could have been a public speaking competition or a big sports match or a bungee jump. When you came out the other side, you were probably very proud of yourself! This proves that you can put yourself in a new and fearful situation and succeed. In her book *Feel The Fear And Do It Anyway*, Susan Jeffers explains that the

feeling doesn't go away and that you just need to feel it and go ahead with whatever you were going to do!

Now that you know the value of trying something new and have some tools for quieting your fear, let's get started on getting you hired. As with any successful business venture, the best place to start is with the employer.

So how do employers think? Well, firstly no one sees himself or herself as an employer. If you ask people what they do for a living, they will not state: "I am an employer." Instead they will say they are a business owner, a managing director, a salesperson, a marketing professional, and so on. Many companies don't have an HR department or a dedicated recruitment team in their business, so most of the time you will be dealing with these people directly. To ensure you don't waste their time, you will need to understand what is important to them specifically.

Even if companies do have an HR department, the final decision will rest with the hiring manger or company director. All of these people involved in the hiring decisions will have their own personal agendas. Just like you and me, these managers are concerned with their own success and reputation. If they manage within the company, it is tied to their own job security or advancement potential. One sure-fire way to get hired is to prove you can help your manager achieve these goals. They want team members who will help them get the job done and make them look good. The more you know about your prospective manager, the better prepared you can be to prove you are the one who can do this.

So how can we find out more about the person interviewing us?

Well, luckily in this day and age we often only have to Google someone's name and we can find all sorts of information. Twitter, Facebook and LinkedIn are also great sources of information.

Hopefully by now you will have completed the personality questionnaire on http://ima-connecting.com and you will have realised that all of us have different personalities. Did you know that it is also true that most jobs have personalities too?

Sales people tend to be 'High Yellow'. They are enthusiastic, passionate and friendly, and thrive on having fun. In an interview it is best to build rapport, share stories and not be too serious. So smile, relax and enjoy the experience! High Yellows want to be surrounded by positive energy and people.

CEOs and **company directors** are often 'High Red'. They like people to get to the point quickly and hate waffle. The best way to impress these people in an interview situation is demonstrate your value and benefits succinctly, tell them you want to work for them and explain how you can help them grow and make money.

IT professionals are often 'High Green'. They are methodical, non-assertive and analytical and like to be presented with lots of facts, data and information.

Caring professionals such as **nurses**, **teachers** and **admin workers** are often 'High Blue'. These people are non-assertive and friendly, and would like it if you built rapport but weren't overly forceful in your approach.

Interestingly, if you Google a potential employer and find his or her name comes up a lot, it is likely he or she is a high yellow. Yellows thrive on attention and love being published or being well known in their industry. If the employer seems more serious from related Twitter feeds and their company title, then they will most likely be a red or a green. Directors in particular are almost always red.

Companies are in business to grow and be profitable. It is very important that you understand this and start positioning yourself in a way that helps the business grow. Going back to my career-coaching games tester example, I taught my client to think about why the games company was in business in the first place. The answer was to create games that customers would want to buy, so they can get more revenue and then profit. A games company doesn't want to produce games that won't sell! Then I asked my client to think about why a games tester would be important in helping the business be profitable. The answers were that he could spot problems and identify any improvements that could be made, helping prevent imperfect games being released, and therefore saving the games company money.

Remembering that a CEO cares about three things (**making money**, **saving money** and **mitigating risk**), you can start positioning yourself in a way that helps the company achieve those goals.

Step 1 – Think about the role itself
By using LinkedIn and searching job boards, start to understand what roles the company has had available in the past and tailor your experience to that role. Try to understand why the role may have become available.

Step 2 – Understand the screening process
The purpose of the screening process is to minimise the amount of applications. A company's screening process will pose the question: who can we get rid of?

A computer or an assistant will quickly screen the CVs for keywords and key skills. Obvious reasons to put them straight in the 'no' pile include poor spelling and grammar, typos or messy appearance. Employers often spend less than a minute per CV before putting it in the 'yes' or 'no' pile.

Next, telephone interviews will be conducted and therefore you need to have a friendly phone manner, and be enthusiastic and focused on the phone. I have rejected countless candidates just from the way the say 'Hello'! Please refer to Chapter 4 for more information on telephone interviews and what employers are looking for.

The above demonstrates why often it is often better to miss the screening process altogether and go straight to the decision maker using the 'side door' method. During my sales career I was always told to cold-call from the top and work my way down, rather than the other harder and slower way of beginning at the bottom and working my way up.

Step 3 – Identify how you can help a company make money, save money and reduce risk

You have to think like employers to know what would screen you out. Once you remember they specifically want to hire people who will make them profitable, this should become easier for you.

Step 4 – Understanding the personality type of the employer and blend in

From your research online, or from any mutual contacts, can you determine what is of interest to them? What is their personal agenda? Using your new emotional intelligence skills gained from iMA, you should be able to pinpoint their personality type and colour, and blending in appropriately should now be an achievable goal.

CHAPTER 8: CONFIDENCE AND THE POWER OF POSITIVE THINKING

"Don't ask yourself what the world needs. Ask yourself what makes you come alive, and then go and do that. Because what the world needs is people who have come alive."
Howard Thurman

Confidence is crucial to success because once you start believing you're 'worth it' then you will follow your passions – believe me, you want to be doing something you're passionate about and interested in, otherwise you won't lead a happy life.

Don't get me wrong, I understand that right now we don't have the best economy, however I also know that if you're confident in your abilities and are proactive enough to go after what you want, then you can and will get your dream job.

WHAT DOES IT MEAN TO BE CONFIDENT?

I have already mentioned the competencies employers look for when taking on graduates, however I am aware that there are a lack of resources teaching graduates how to display and develop these competencies. I have included a number of hints and tips below describing how to improve your confidence, add value, display positivity and much more.

The reason employers value confidence is because it suggests a fast learner, who can adapt to new situations quickly and easily, and will not be intimidated when speaking to clients and internal team members. This is very valuable and beneficial because it means the graduate will take less time to train. The biggest reason employers don't hire graduates is because they don't have time to train them.

Some hints and tips on how to 'fake it until you make it' and appear confident are as follows:

1. **It's all in the body language** – As I advised in Chapter 6, if you're at an interview waiting for the employer, stand up in reception, rather than sitting down. Make sure you are looking at pictures or reading the provided literature whilst standing, as it will appear as if you are waiting confidently. Putting your hands behind your back or standing with a straight back are also signs of self-confidence.

2. **Be relaxed** – Confident people are relaxed and can handle criticism. They don't bite their nails or wait anxiously. The best way to be relaxed in an interview is to prepare, prepare and prepare! If you can predict what questions you will be asked and are prepared with the best answers then you have every reason to be confident and relaxed. I would prepare by writing down the top ten reasons that company should hire you, so you understand your strengths, and also the top ten reasons why someone wouldn't hire you. By writing the reasons someone wouldn't hire you, you will be prepared for the 'objection' and will have an answer to overcome it.

3. **Smile and be animated** – Unconfident people tend to not want to be noticed and are quiet. Confident people on the other hand value an audience and are very enthusiastic

and animated. The best way to display animation and enthusiasm is to smile. This will trick your subconscious mind into believing you are feeling confident and happy, and that is how you will appear. Another trick is to raise your voice when speaking.

4. **Be assertive** – Assertiveness can be displayed with a clear and strong tone of voice, a structure to your interview answers, no waffle, being direct and getting to the point. My FEATURE, PROOF, BENEFIT rule acts as a great guide for structuring your answers to appear more assertive. The Feature is 'I have great communication skills', the Proof is an example of how this has been demonstrated, i.e. 'I was chosen by my school to represent them in all the public speaking competitions throughout the borough' and the Benefit is a reason why this company should care, for example, 'this means that I can confidently liaise with your customers with ease and deliver an exceptional customer service.'

5. **Remain calm when criticised** – Confident people accept criticism with a smile. They empathise and agree with the other person's point of view and then overcome the objection in a logical and professional way.

Another tip I mention regularly is that employers are looking to hire graduates who can add value. What this means is it is important to put yourself into the employer's shoes and think about their business objectives, how they want to achieve growth and what they need to make that happen. If you can go to the interview with knowledge of that company's key strengths, weaknesses, opportunities and threats (a SWOT analysis), then you can pinpoint where you may be able to help them improve their weakness and grow.

The employer will be really impressed with your additional research and you can continue to explain how you can go the extra mile to add value to their business.

HOW DO YOU BECOME MORE CONFIDENT?

Confidence is a quality that truly comes from within. While it is possible to fake it as described as above, it is something you need to believe in.

Firstly you need to love yourself – remember you are a fantastic creature, so focus on your strengths. Are you a good writer? Do you have excellent maths skills? Are you friendly and kind? Are you a good listener, or a better salesperson? Think about your good qualities and the positive aspects of YOU. Everyone has positive traits. Think of your abilities and past accomplishments. Identify those people who like you, look up to and respect you. Include aspects of yourself you like, such as character traits, talents and achievements. Write down those skills you possess naturally or have developed and always continue adding to your list of positives. Benjamin Franklin did this. By focusing on your strengths and not dwelling on your weaknesses, you will slowly become more confident.

ARE WE BORN LUCKY?

How is it that some people seem to breeze through life, find their perfect partner, enjoy the perfect career, achieve all their personal goals and always seem to get lucky breaks when others are consistently unlucky? What is it that the lucky people have or do that the unlucky people don't? Modern society may suggest that luck comes about from looks or certain personality traits or it is something you're born with, however there is far more to it than that.

In his book *The Luck Factor*, Dr Richard Wiseman delves into this topic in great detail. In his research of hundreds of 'lucky' and 'unlucky people', he has discovered that there are four characteristics naturally lucky people possess. These are:

1. **'Being in the right place at the right time'** – Lucky people create, notice and act upon the chance opportunities in their life. Each of us is presented with an abundance of chance opportunities, but it is just the 'lucky' people who see them and act upon them, while the 'unlucky' people don't. Therefore the phrase 'being in the right place at the right time' is really just a matter of being in the right state of mind.

2. **'Listen to your lucky hunches'** – Lucky people make successful decisions by using their intuition and gut feelings. Albert Einstein famously wrote, "There is only the way of intuition." Lucky people actually make steps to improving their intuition by meditating.

3. **'Expect good fortune'** – Lucky people's expectations about the future help them fulfil their dreams and ambitions. Lucky people naturally just expect their good luck to continue in the future! They set out to achieve their goals, even if their chance of success is slim. They persevere in the face of failure.

4. **'Turn bad luck into good'** – Lucky people see the positive side of their bad luck. They are convinced that any ill fortune in their lives will work out for the best.

To summarise, if you start seeing the bright side of life, you will start feeling the effects of the bright side of life. Begin today and see how you feel!

How to be positive

So much is written about the power of positive thinking. It is somehow believed that if we consciously change a negative thought to a positive thought, then miraculously our lives will change for the better. And even though we know we should be positive, sometimes it is really hard isn't it? You didn't get the job, your friend didn't return your phone call, the car broke down, your cat died. Things happen all the time to put us in a bad mood, so how can we be positive? Because, quite frankly, just changing our belief system isn't working!

This is because positivity goes deeper and takes a lot more effort than just changing a thought. It is about remembering that these unconscious negative patterns reoccur because our brain has created mini 'bear traps' which wait until the thought comes in again, traps it and then re-confirms that our thought was right. The only way you can trick the 'bear traps' and remove them is by focusing on how you *want* to feel instead.

All the possibilities are here in a world of no fear!

What would happen if you didn't watch the news? Well, you may not know what was going on in the world, but would that be such a bad thing? Imagine not knowing there was a recession; imagine not knowing about the dangers occurring in the world. Would living in a bubble bring some benefits?

The one thing that prevents most of us from making changes and doing what we want to do is **fear**. And where does fear come from? Yes, you've guessed it! Fear comes from the fact that we get bombarded everyday by the media that the world is a scary place, that you shouldn't travel alone, that you must stay in your job because there are no other jobs out there, that you must not spend your money, etc., etc.

As an experiment, I want you to spend two weeks not watching or listening to the news. Imagine a world filled with opportunity and jobs for graduates. When you start to switch off from the 'noise' filling our subconscious minds around us, it opens you up to possibilities and will alleviate your fear.

Whatever you want to do you *can* achieve. No one is any different or better than anyone else. If you want something that someone else has, then find out how they have got to where they are and 'model' or 'copy' it.

If you take yourself out of the world you are in (the quickest and easiest way being to avoid watching TV) then you are free to create your own world. You will have no fear, no preconception and you will have time to learn from other fearless people, join their ranks and become part of their society.

I can guarantee you that if you interview all the successful people in the world the majority will have created their own mini worlds and haven't listened or been affected by the media and coverage that the masses hold onto as the truth. They will have created their own worlds full of possibility and will believe that anything is possible.

In *Feel The Fear And Do It Anyway*, Susan Jeffers talks about this point and tells us to accept the fear, remember it is most likely unwarranted and then go ahead and achieve what you want to achieve.

Give it a try; you have nothing to lose.

THE POWER OF THE SUBCONSCIOUS WITH IMPROVING CONFIDENCE AND POSITIVITY

The other morning I walked into a gym in LA. There was no one on reception so I walked in confidently with my head held high, and acted like I belonged there. The receptionist then came back, and shot me a 'look', suggesting that he knew I hadn't registered. However, because I was so confident, I tricked his subconscious mind into believing that I belonged and he let me stay. This is the second time this has happened! I also have a free gym membership in London. I walk in and in true Derren Brown style I hand over my card (a card I haven't refilled for three months) and they let me in. I know this is primarily due to the fact that because I go so often, they believe I belong there and that I am definitely a member and they let me in. I have tricked their subconscious into believing I belong.

So what is the point of this story? And what does this mean for you and how it can help you in everyday life? The point is that **confidence is perceived**. If you act confident, internally and externally, then people will believe that you are. As confidence has such a positive effect on people, then this is an incredibly important skill. People will perceive you to be more capable, stronger, and more reliable. They will warm to you and trust you. They will believe that you will complete everything you say you will. Moreover, in a job situation, they will want to hire you! In my case, my confidence demonstrated that I must have belonged; I must have had a gym membership.

So how do you improve your confidence? The trick is to 'model excellence', i.e. think of people, famous or not, whom you consider 'confident' and analyse how they carry themselves. What you'll find is they walk with their heads held high, shoulders back and have a calm face. They won't waffle and instead will get to the point quickly and easily. They will be very well presented and they will listen attentively to everything they are asked before responding. They will also be knowledgeable and intelligent.

One trick to speed your confidence and become the person that people perceive to be capable and belong anywhere is to meditate every morning for 5-10 minutes to clear your mind from clutter and present a calm demeanour.

To feel confident and positive in everyday life, find an outfit that you feel very smart in. I recommend a nice pair of jeans, smart shoes and a smart jacket for both boys and girls. A suit can look too forced and uncomfortable, unless you are heading for an interview, or your workplace demands it. Jewellery and make-up should be kept to a minimum (perhaps discrete earrings, a necklace and a watch).

Practice listening and asking questions, rather than talking. People like people like themselves and people like talking about themselves, so make others feel important and you will invite positive reactions. If necessary, repeat the mantra 'You belong here, you are important' in your head to install into your subconscious mind. You have to truly believe that you belong and then other people will believe too.

This confidence trick can be used to get into guest-only events, VIP sections, the front of queues and, of course, into gyms...

All you need to do is believe!

HOW TO BE HAPPY

Recently I suffered another traumatic event in my life. I could feel the familiar pattern of pain returning to my body and mind and I felt I was about to tumble down the rabbit hole. Fortunately for me, I became consciously aware that my old patterns were returning, and I sought help at just the right time. After this episode, I was determined to learn how to be happy, even when going through trauma. The last thing I wanted was to fall into depression and I wanted to know if there was another way.

This led me to meet <u>Dr. Aymee Coget</u>, a leading authority on happiness who was described by the New York Times as the Suze Orman of happiness, who states that 'one can teach happiness just like we teach math'. I was intrigued, and I wanted to learn how, so I could teach myself and other people how to live their happiest lives.

I have been working with Aymee now for 12+ months and I am half way through her magical happiness makeover program and I am the happiest I have ever been. The last 12 months have been wonderful, and this is because I have adopted a few techniques into my daily routine that has helped me re-train my brain and become a positive, happy person. The great news is you can easily incorporate these techniques into your lives also!

Step 1- Adopt a happiness routine. I must admit, I really enjoy being given a formula to follow to produce results, so having a daily routine really appealed to me. I follow a structured routine at the gym and at work to produce my best results, so it made sense that I would have to follow a formula to re-program my mind. I begin every day with Aymee's morning routine. Here is a <u>fun video of Aymee doing the morning routine</u> a few years ago for Blogher... it may make you smile and laugh... :)

Step 2- Express Gratitude- People who regularly practice gratitude by taking time to notice and reflect upon the things they're thankful for experience more positive emotions, feel more alive, sleep better, express more compassion and kindness, and even have stronger immune systems. <u>Research</u> by UC Davis psychologist Robert Emmons, author of *Thanks!: How the New Science of Gratitude Can Make You Happier*, shows that simply keeping a gratitude journal—regularly writing brief reflections on moments for which we're thankful—can significantly increase well-being and life satisfaction.

Step 3- Move daily- Every day brings with it a new scientific report on the benefits of exercise and sometimes the overload of information can be overwhelming. The great news is moving for just 20 minutes a day will help you feel your happiest self. This includes walking! As a new mum I hardly have any time for myself, however, I always incorporate 20-30 mins of yoga (<u>check out 30 days of yoga with Adriene on Youtube</u>) or a walk every day.

Step 4- Watch your language- As a Master NLP Practitioner (<u>Tony Robbins</u> is the most famous authority on NLP), I have learned the impact of our words on our subconscious minds and how they formulate our beliefs and our actions. Interestingly, although I know in theory how it all works, cutting out negative language was very difficult for me. Aymee wanted me to cut the words 'No', 'Not', 'Can't', 'Won't', 'Should', 'But' and 'Try' out of my language repertoire. Although I am yet to perfect this, I can see the results are already life changing!

Step 5- Live in the moment. 'Living in the moment means letting go of the past and not waiting for the future. It means living your life consciously, aware that each moment you breathe is a gift' **Oprah Winfrey.** The easiest way to live in the moment is to ask your senses what is happening right now. For example, every few minutes (you can get a vibrating watch to remind you) check in with your senses and ask 'what do I see?', 'what can I hear?', 'What can I smell?/taste?/feel? in this moment?. In the beginning, you may have to do this exercise 100 times per day, however, once you practice it gets easier. I also start or end the day with a guided meditation. There are tons of apps now (headspace, calm) and you can find loads of guided meditations on YouTube. A great trick is to listen to an app on your commute to work or fall asleep to one whilst lying in bed.

Step 6- Conduct 5 random acts of kindness daily- Giving back to others is the best way to feel happy. A random act of kindness can be anything from reaching out to a friend, to buying a homeless person a coffee, to providing a larger tip than normal or writing a handwritten card to someone you care about. I promise you the more you give back to others, the happier you will feel.

Step 7- Catch your negative thoughts and reframe them- Tony Robbins states that 'the level of success we experience internally- the happiness, joy, ecstasy, love or anything else we desire- is the direct result of how we communicate to ourselves". If you find yourself having negative thoughts, catch them and write them down. Once you have written the thought down, on the opposite side of the page, re-frame that thought and write down the positive. For example, 'I hate myself' becomes 'I love myself'. At night, you will then read all the positive thoughts to yourself before bed.

Step 8- Eat healthy foods- "Came from a plant, eat it; was made in a plant, don't." -*Michael Pollan*. I really believe everything in moderation and you should have the odd treat now and again, however, it is important to eat healthy, nutritious foods to feel your best, most happy self.

THE POWER OF NETWORKING

Can you imagine a world filled with an abundance of job opportunities, free 'guest list only' parties, an opportunity to travel the world and free food and drink? Well, all this can be possible with the power of networking.

Networking means meeting people, building rapport, getting them to warm to you and creating opportunities.

Networking requires an ability to connect with people. Regrettably, even at business schools, little of the educational experience seems to address this issue or teach the necessary 'people skills' to get ahead.

It makes sense. As Zig Ziglar says, "You don't build a business – you build people – and then people build the business." When you go for a job, walk into a party, or, in fact, go anywhere, you're coming into contact with *people*. So how can you connect with people and get them to like you, thereby creating all the amazing opportunities you would want?

Well, other than by employing the teachings of iMA regarding emotional intelligence (see Chapter 7 and Appendix 1), it is important to remember the point that Dale Carnegie made in *How To Win Friends And Influence People* that, "people like to feel important". What is the easiest way of making people feel important? It is by listening to them and empathising with their point of view. If you listen to other people, let them speak, understand and empathise with their point of view, then they will warm to you and like you.

I have mentioned several times in this book that 96% of what we do, think and feel is subconscious, meaning that a large proportion of our beliefs, values and morals have been formed subconsciously and have been influenced by our parents, our friends, our school, our university, the media, etc. When we meet people, they give us lots of clues about what beliefs they might have and some level of understanding about their unique map and model of the world. The clothes they wear, the way they speak, their accent, their non-verbal gestures, the way they walk all present some clues as to what they may be like.

With this in mind, you can tailor your personality to suit all people. This is a brilliant skill when networking. Let the other person speak, be interested in what he or she has to say, don't interrupt and then build rapport by demonstrating **common interests**. Being supportive and interested in other people's points of view will translate towards them wanting to be around you. More importantly, they will want to connect you to opportunities that can help in some way.

Networking is a fantastic skill to learn for when you are applying for jobs. Remember, you are not applying for a job with a company; you are applying for a job with a person! The company is just a name that has been registered with company's house. It is people that built that business, therefore you need to have the 'people skills' to get the job. So put yourself into other people's shoes, demonstrate empathy and people will respond to that. Give these tools a try at your next networking event and see what a difference it makes!

"Networking is a fantastic skill to learn for when you are applying for jobs. Remember, you are not applying for a job with a company; you are applying for a job with a person!"

Networking is primarily all about who we know and who *they* know. Healthy business relationships are always based on like and trust, because when this occurs, your contacts will want to help you. By asking for assistance or advice when you are job searching, you flatter their egos and are essentially paying them a compliment. By asking for references or LinkedIn referrals, you pay tribute to their standing and knowledge base.

One thing to remember: when a contact helps you, try not to leave the meeting without asking for names of two or three further contacts of theirs. As Will Kintish explains, "At the end of the day it's a numbers game, whether looking for business or a new job."

CHAPTER 9: TIPS FROM THE TOP

WHAT EMPLOYERS WANT – A SUMMARY

In this final chapter I want to recap on the key points explored within this book ... what employers are actually looking for!

All employers seek:

1. **Someone who can add value** – An employer will be investing money and time into hiring a graduate and therefore you must be able to demonstrate how you can add value to them. Your employer will be in business to make money, save money and mitigate risk, so start positioning yourself in those terms. Think about how you can help make the company money (perhaps conducting research into potential customers, booking meetings for their top sales closers to attend, dealing with admin to free up the time of the senior members of the team, giving great customer service to existing customers). Think about how you can save them money (you will cost a lot less than experienced members of the team, you are a fast learner and can assimilate information quickly) and then discuss how and why you are low risk. For example, you may have a great academic record, you can demonstrate you understand their industry, you don't need much time to train, etc.

2. **Someone positive with a great attitude** – Potential employers want to be surrounded by positive energy and

by confident people who will remain upbeat even when the going gets tough. Business is not easy and mistakes will be made along the way. You need to be someone who has encountered rejection before and handled it well. You must be strong, resilient and positive.

3. **Someone who can be taught quickly and easily** – Time is a precious commodity in business and employers will want to employ a candidate who won't take up too much of their time. Demonstrate that you are obsessed by your own personal development and learning. Visit the library, your old university careers centre, bookshops or research on the Internet to learn everything you can about their industry and competitors. Conduct a SWOT analysis and read books on personal growth and self-development.

4. **Someone who will take the initiative** – At university you spent hours writing essays and dissertations on subjects which you may or may not concentrate on in the working world. Why not take all that knowledge you have gained and begin a dissertation on the company you are going for an interview with? Prepare a document demonstrating their strengths and your suggestions for them to improve. The employer will be incredibly impressed with the initiative shown.

5. **Someone confident** – Once you understand that 96% of what people think and feel is subconscious, you can play to this and realise that if you act confident, the person interviewing you will perceive you as confident. This means that they will consider you as someone who will get the job done and conduct yourself appropriately.

6. **Someone intelligent** – Employers want to know that they can trust you to write emails and letters without any

mistakes. They want to trust you to discuss key initiatives and propose intelligent ideas and suggestions. They want to groom you to be a potential leader of the company, and therefore intelligence is key! Portray this from the very beginning with a well-structured CV free from spelling mistakes and typos.

7. **Someone presentable** – In business, especially in customer-facing roles, presentation is very important. Employers want to be certain that you will represent their organisation with professionalism when the office doors have shut and that you will be a great spokesperson for their company.

8. **Someone who is focused and can clearly demonstrate they want the job** – Everyone is egocentric and the best way to get a job is by clearly voicing that this is the industry, company and job that you want. Never say that you are going for interviews with everyone and anyone. Stroke the ego, state that this is the only role you want, and tailor your CV accordingly.

There are so many suggestions you can implement now if you want to maximise your chances. Focus on what you want and position yourself as an expert in that area; study the industry and write a SWOT analysis for every interview you go too; smarten up. Get a haircut, buy a new suit, polish your shoes, and start practising being more confident. Hold your head high, walk with your shoulders back and repeat a positive mantra to yourself as you walk.

SHOULD YOU CONSIDER COACHING?

"Go confidently in the direction of your dreams! Live the life you've imagined.
As you simplify your life, the laws of the universe will be simpler."
Henry David Thoreau

The word 'coaching' seems to be bandied everywhere these days and there has definitely been a rise of coaches in the UK. A rise is always followed by a demand, so what exactly is coaching and how can it benefit you?

Life coaching has long been a television staple, with coaches helping sort out the lives of single men, ugly ducklings, sexually unsatisfied wives and others in shows like *The Swan*, *Starting Over* and *Modern Men*. Life coaches, with their vague 'self-help' title, have also come in for considerable scepticism and ribbing. So what is coaching and how does it differ from psychotherapy?

Explains Phil Towle, a psychotherapist and life coach: "The difference between life coaching and therapy is that psychotherapy is about helping people heal their wounds, and coaching is about helping people achieve the highest level of their fulfilment or happiness or success, whether they're wounded or not."

To put it more simply, life coaching is specifically for those people **willing** and **wanting** to make inner and outer changes in their lives.

Successful people hire coaches. Indeed, coaching is a secret that some of the most successful business people share. Hiring a coach is one of the best things you can do for yourself in business. Guess what? It's also one of the best things you can do for your personal life. Coaching in the area of money, career, improved communication skills, weight loss, dating and relationships can help you reach your goals much faster than you would on your own. Getting the insights of a coach can help you overcome the obstacles that you encounter in daily life.

Read the dream versus reality points below and remember a coach can turn your dreams into your reality!

- **DREAM:** Financially independent with money in savings – **REALITY**: living on a credit card

- **DREAM:** Volunteering to help those in need – **REALITY:** Accepting free lodging and food yourself

- **DREAM:** Travelling the world – **REALITY:** Staring at the office walls

- **DREAM:** Fitting into skinny jeans – **REALITY:** Telling yourself the diet starts tomorrow

- **DREAM:** Being in a loving relationship with your best friend – **REALITY:** Dating losers who just aren't that into you

- **DREAM:** Putting your hard earned degree to use – **REALITY:** Wondering what the purpose of going to university was

- **DREAM:** Travelling on your company's expense – **REALITY:** Working overtime without pay

- **DREAM:** Feeling included, appreciated and inspired – **REALITY:** Huh? What?

- **DREAM:** Being confident of your direction and purpose – **REALITY:** I have no idea what my purpose is

- **DREAM:** Living on your own – **REALITY:** Living in a flat share

Whether you're seeking straightforward career coaching, or whether you're stuck in a rut and need motivation, have a decision to make but don't know the right way to go, want to and reaching goals, then a coach can help you.

Another great reason to hire a coach is to help you overcome your past self-limiting beliefs. In my experience the reason why so many people struggle to achieve their goals is because of events that have occurred in the past. Our past conditioning creates self-limiting beliefs and the only way to 'clear' these beliefs is through NLP (Neuro-Linguistic Programming). When coaches are trained in NLP and hypnotherapy, they are able to work with clients on clearing their blocks so they can successfully achieve all their goals.

Our beliefs lie at the core of who we are. Beliefs guide our decisions and behaviour in all areas of life. They determine what we think is or is not possible. More often than not, they prove to be self-fulfilling prophecies. Some of our beliefs are not fully our own, but rather blindly taken on from others. Once a belief is formed, we work overtime to prove it right, even if the belief is something negative like, "Nobody likes me," or, "I am a failure." The great news is you don't have to let your beliefs govern you and you can consciously make changes to what you believe. This is what life coaching mixed with NLP can do for you.

In the first half of the 20th century the world believed that it was impossible to run a mile under four minutes. When, on May 6th 1954, Roger Bannister ran a mile in 3:59 minutes, everyone was in awe. Then, a curious development took place. Within the following year many other runners also ran the mile in under four minutes. It was as if a spell had been broken. Suddenly the belief was changed to 'it was possible' and this created results.

Some of the beliefs we hold give us great strength and empowerment. Studies show that, on average, people who believe they are healthy live seven years longer than those who think they are unhealthy, regardless of their actual health condition at the time of the survey.

Other beliefs zap our energy. They tell us that we cannot achieve our goals or that we are not worthy of other people's acceptance. Those kinds of beliefs are called 'Limiting Beliefs' in NLP. They typically sound like, "I am ugly", "I will never be successful," and "I can't work with those people."

It is these beliefs that stand between you and your goal.

If you would like to learn more about Coaching Services, go to www.theapprenticeproject.com and add a contact request.

IF AT FIRST YOU DON'T SUCCEED ... WHAT IF YOU CAN'T FIND A JOB?

The information contained within this book is designed to give you a head start over other graduates who are in exactly the same position as you. I have every confidence that, if you follow my hints and tips, you will be successful in obtaining the job of your dreams much sooner than if you hadn't invested in *The Graduate Bible*.

However, if you have spent a long time looking for but not finding a job, then it might be time to explore some other options, including:

1. Considering an alternative career

2. Furthering your education

3. Re-evaluating your CV and interview skills

4. Changing your timing, for example by reapplying when you have developed new skills or gained certain experience

5. Requesting informational interviews

6. Finding an internship

7. Taking on temporary assignments and/or part-time work – these will boost your CV

8. Starting your own business – think of something that can solve a problem or fulfil a need

9. Seeking out freelance or contract work

10. Changing locations – whether you are job searching from home, in a library or in a coffee shop, you can gain a fresh perspective when you change your environment

11. Talking with others – ask other people how they conducted their job search and how they became successful

Remember, you are a **product** and it's time to market yourself! Devise your own personal marketing plan, which involves researching your target market to learn more about jobs, key personnel and industry trends. Then remember that, as with all products, **packaging is important**. See yourself as a gift. You are smart, motivated, capable, and ambitious. Position yourself appropriately within the **market**, consider your **pricing** (salary starting level) and even the **copy** (words) used to describe yourself in your social media profiles, blog, CV, application forms and introductory emails.

Above all, try to relax and enjoy the next stage of your career. You've put many years of hard work into getting to this position, so be proud of yourself and have fun embarking on the next steps. I wish you all the luck in the world on your graduate journey into employment.

Emma Vites, BA

APPENDIX 1: IMA PERSONALITY DEFINITIONS AND DESCRIPTIONS

Following on from **Chapter 7 – How to be more emotionally intelligent**, hopefully by now you will have visited http://ima-connecting.com and completed the online personality questionnaire. Read on to find out more about your iMA colour and discover how to connect with the other three colours on the spectrum.

HIGH YELLOWS

People who are Right Brain Thinking and Assertive are High Yellows.

Description

High Yellows are chatty, expressive fun-loving optimists. They are fast-paced, energetic and outgoing. They deal with others in an upbeat way. They love an audience and being where the action is. They are friendly, enthusiastic and gregarious, and thrive on admiration, acknowledgments, and compliments.

They like:
- Brainstorming and generating fresh ideas

- To get others excited about their vision

- Being personally involvement

- To be involved with groups rather than independent activities

- To avoid serious issues, and deflect pain with humour

- Work that provides variety and plenty of opportunities to interact with others

- An audience and they thrive on involvement

They dislike:
- Things that move too slow

- Tedium and routine

- Boring tasks

- Being alone

- Not having access to a telephone

- Being around negative people

- Decisions being made without them

When things move too slowly, or if the emphasis is too much on tasks, this can cause High Yellows stress. They may become:

- Argumentative

- Opinionated

- Overconfident

- Over eager

- Manipulative

- Wasteful of time

- Unrealistic

- Superficial

- Impulsive

- Inconsistent

- Likely to make excuses

Their strengths include:
- Enthusiasm

- Charm

- Persuasiveness

- Warmth

- They are eternal optimists, with an abundance of charisma

- They are 'ideas' people who gets others excited about their visions

- They are able to get along with many types of people

- They create a positive expectancy in others

- They tend to see both sides of an argument

- They have a dynamic ability to think quickly on their feet

- They are true entertainers

- They work quickly and enthusiastically with others

- They are quick to adapt new ideas and approaches

Their weaknesses include:
- They may spend too much time socialising and not completing tasks

- They may get scattered into many different directions

- They may side-track serious discussions and appear superficial

- They may dilute messages so that the receiver does not understand the seriousness of a problem

- They may appear flighty and melodramatic, and they might be inconsistent

To be more effective, High Yellows should:
- Be more objective in making decisions

- Develop more organised, systematic approaches to tasks

- Improve follow-through by attending to key details

- Learn to be direct and firm in confrontation

- Exert more control over the use of time

HIGH BLUES

People who are Right Brain Thinking and Non-Assertive are High Blues.

Description
High Blues are pleasant, cooperative team players, great listeners, devoted friends and loyal employees. They are supportive and nurturing individuals. High Blues are the most people-oriented of the four iMA styles.

High Blues' relaxed disposition makes them approachable and warm. They develop a strong network of people who are willing to be mutually supportive and reliable.

They like:
- Things to move in a slow, relaxed pace

- To share personal feelings and emotions

- Close personal long-term, in-depth relationships

- To work with others as a team

- The status quo

- A productive routine

- Tranquillity and stability at work/home

- To avoid conflict

- Being involved with groups

- To make decisions slowly

- Sincere feedback

- To be appreciated

- A step-by-step sequence of projects and tasks

- To have everything in place before they get started

- To work slowly and cohesively with others

- Informality/to deal on a first name basis

- To ask a lot of questions

- To be involved with people

- Everyone to do their share

- For things to run smoothly

- To be involved in completing tasks

- To do things to help people

- Others to be pleasant and to support their feelings

They dislike:
- Things moving too fast

- The emphasis to be too much on tasks, rather than relationships

- Pushy aggressive people

- Interpersonal conflict

- Disruptions to their routine

- Change and want to do it only a little at a time

- Insensitive people

The above can cause High Blues stress and they may:
- Withdraw

- Turn inward

- Lack energy

They may appear:
- Passive

- Dependent

- Hesitant

- Defensive

- Indecisive

High Blue strengths include:

- They are very easy to get along with

- They are personable, trustworthy, likable, loyal, reliable

- They have a relaxed disposition

- They accept people as they are

- They are very approachable

- Patience and consideration in dealing with others

- Developing strong networks of people

- Natural counselling skills

- Being extremely supportive

- They are very dependable

- They bring a calming influence within a group

- Their ability to gain the support of others

- They are great team players

- They are good planners and persistent workers

Every iMA style has strengths and limiting patterns of behaviour and weaknesses often times grow out of strengths. For High Blues perceived weaknesses include:

- Indecisiveness

- Trouble saying "no"

- Over committing their time and energy

- Being too trusting

- Having difficulty delegating

- Having difficulty taking a firm stand

- Making too many concessions

- Backing down from necessary confrontations in the name of harmony

To increase effectiveness High Blues need to
- Say 'no' occasionally

- Be willing to reach beyond their comfort zone

- Attend to the completion of tasks without oversensitivity to others' feelings

- Take a few risks

- Learn to handle change better

- Become more assertive

- Increase their comfort with open conflict

- Vary routines occasionally

- Become more receptive to shortcut methods

- Speak up when they are concerned or upset

HIGH REDS

People that are Left Brain Thinking and Assertive are High Reds.

Description

High Reds are fast-paced, task oriented goal setting go-getters that are most comfortable in control of people and situations. They are cool, independent competitive, accept challenges, take authority and go headlong into solving problems.

High Reds are great administrators, delegators and doers. They can move mountains; people are in awe of their ability to figure out what needs to be done and then to do it.

They like to:

- Overcome obstacles

- Take control of people and situations

- Exhibit firmness in relationship with others

- Juggle three things at once, and when they're comfortable, pick up a fourth

- Deal quickly with practical problems

- Work quickly by themselves

- Change, often self-initiated

- To work hard and often

- Thrive on crisis and controversy

- To display a killer instinct and beat the odds

- A no-nonsense approach to bottom line results

- A fast pace, new projects, change and variety

- Challenges and competition

They dislike:

- Small talk

- Delays

- People that talk about producing results then don't do it

- Wasting time

- Touchy-feely people

- Others that are not as able or motivated as they are

- Inefficiency and indecision

- Weakness in others and themselves

- Inaction

- Losing control over the environment

- Boredom

- Being tied to routine

- Being taken advantage of

This may cause them stress and they become:

- Pushy

- Aggressive

- Critical

- Blunt

- Intrusive

- Uncooperative

- Irritable

High Red strengths include:

- The ability to get things done

- Leadership skills

- Decision-making skills

- Moving forcefully to generate results

- Being self-sufficient

- Being quick to confront conflicts

- Being highly competitive

- Being quick to act

- Work impressively by themselves

- Accepting challenges

- Jumping headlong into solving problems

- A matter of fact, to the point communicating style

Every iMA style has strengths and limiting patterns of behaviour. Weaknesses often grow out of strengths. For High Reds they can:

- Appear abrasive

- Not acknowledge other people very much

- Find others may question their compassion

- Overpower others

- Find others may feel pressured

- Be seen as blunt and uncaring

To be more effective, High Reds need to:
- Practice active listening

- Pace themselves to project a more relaxed image

- Develop patience, humility and sensitivity and concern for others' needs

- Use more caution

- Verbalise the reasons for conclusions

- Identify with the group

HIGH GREENS

People who are Left Brain Thinking and Non-Assertive are High Greens.

Description:
High Greens are analytical, persistent and systematic people who enjoy problem solving. They are logical, well-organised, task-oriented people who work slowly and methodically to produce accurate systems. They enjoy perfecting processes and working towards tangible results. They love logic, adore accuracy and cherish efficiency, and are patient, courteous and thorough.

They like:
- An environment that is neat and tidy

- To work at a slow pace to allow time to process all the information provided

- To work alone and focus on facts, data and processes

- Organisation and structure

- People to be precise, credible, professional and courteous

- Problem-solving

- Perfecting processes

- To set high expectations for themselves and for others

- To know how things work

- Working towards tangible results

- Working within existing guidelines to produce quality goods and services

They dislike
- Things moving too fast

- Threats to accuracy

- Making impulsive decisions

- Too much involvement

- Surprises and glitches

- Disorganised and illogical people

This may cause them stress and they may:
- Withdraw

- Build a shell around themselves

- Withhold cooperation

They may appear
- To be over reliant on data and documentation

- To resist change

- Slow to act

- Slow to begin work

- Unable to meet deadlines

- To lack imagination

- To become resentful

They are:
- Precise

- Efficient

- Accurate

- Independent

- Structured

- Well-organised

- Time disciplined

- Persistent

- Great with follow-through

- Good listeners

- In control of their emotions

- Very good at problem solving

- Very good at establishing systems

High Greens' strengths include:
- Having an eye for detail

- Perfecting processes

- Analysing situations, assessing pros and cons

- Time management and prioritisation

High Greens are inventive, creative intellectuals.

- They are good at perfecting systems and processes

- They make rational decisions based on evidence and are logical and systematic in their approach to situations and tasks

- They develop their own system for managing performance

- They have a high expectation of themselves and others

- They respond calmly to others' objections and concerns

- They present pros and cons of each situation

- They think through possible negative consequences of others' actions

- They set high standards for quality and accuracy

Every iMA style has strengths and limiting patterns of behaviour. Weaknesses often times grow out of strengths. High Greens' weaknesses include:

- They can get stuck in analysis paralysis

- They may have difficulty responding as quickly as needed

- They may have difficulty valuing other people's systems

- They may respond harshly to human imperfection

- They may be perceived as lacking interest or involvement

- They may confuse others with too many options

- They may become rigid and perfectionistic

To increase effectiveness, High Greens need to:
- Openly show concern and appreciation for others

- Occasionally try shortcuts and time savers

- Try to adjust more rapidly to change and disorganisation

- Work on timely decision making and initiating projects

- Compromise with the opposition

- State unpopular decisions

How to modify and adapt to other personality types

Your happiness, effectiveness and future are determined by how well you connect with other people. This in turn depends on your **Adaptability**.

An Adaptable person:

- Meets others' needs as well as his/her own

- Is tactful

- Is reasonable

- Is understanding

- Is non-judgmental

- Is comfortable to talk to

- Is flexible

The Key to Success is Adaptability:

- Treating the other person the way he/she wants to be treated

- Increasing communication

- Increasing trust

- Increasing co-operation

- Reducing tension

An Adaptable person is:

- Confident (i.e. has trust in his/her own judgement)

- Tolerant (i.e. doesn't tend to judge opinions or practices that are different to his/her own)

- Positive ... about other people, situations and life

- Empathetic (i.e. understands what others are feeling and how they want to be treated)

APPENDIX 2: THE MAGIC 'GIVE ME A JOB' LETTER

Will Kintish has kindly given me permission to reprint the following sample letter from his excellent networking content and newsletter (http://www.kintish.co.uk). Use this when approaching companies directly in search of the hidden job market.

Your address

Target address

Date

Dear ....

My name is ....

And the best way to contact me is on...............................

Between now and *[insert reasonable date]* I wish to be working for you as a ....

The reason being is your company *[say something about them showing you have done your research. This bit can make all the difference so spend time on it]*

....

I want this position because *[this is where you tell the reader what sort of a person you are. Use some or all of these]*

- I am enthusiastic about ....
- I have a passion for..
- I enjoy...
- I get absorbed in..
- I am fascinated by...

I am suited for your company/this position because I am good at *[don't be modest if you are particularly good at something]*

- ....
- ....

When you take me on you will find someone who .... *[add something new]*

Finally I want you to know *[a powerful end is vital]* ....

I enclose my CV and look forward to hearing you could grant me an interview or, at least, an informal chat in the first instance.

Yours sincerely,

Signature

Attachments

Wherever possible, attach some references from any sort of previous job you've had, and/or your CV

APPENDIX 3: CASE STUDIES

In this section I thought it would be helpful to include some interviews I used in my research from this book and some advice I have received from friends. These four 'case studies' provide a little insight into some potential careers and job titles for your consideration.

SENIOR IT CONSULTANT - LOUISA PATEL

INDUSTRY: IT
WHAT DOES YOUR ROLE INVOLVE?
I work for a variety of clients, advising them of IT solutions to business issues. I specialise in project management and sourcing, which means that I can be doing anything from implementing new applications to driving down contracts for telephony, to saving organisations millions of pounds.

WHAT ATTRIBUTES ARE IMPORTANT TO HAVE FOR YOUR JOB?
If you want to work in IT, you have to be able to build rapport with lots of different people quickly, as you are constantly creating and leading temporary teams. You need to be flexible and confident so that you can work in different specialist areas. I'm not an IT expert as I did my degree in economics, but you have to be able to pick up some elements of technical information and translate them to managers. Most importantly, you have to be driven as the job changes constantly and you need to be focused on delivery.

HOW DID YOU GET STARTED IN THIS INDUSTRY?
In my final year of university I attended the 'milk round'

presentation of companies and decided to apply online to Fujitsu Services as they were doing a graduate scheme.

WHAT ADVICE WOULD YOU GIVE TO A RECENT GRADUATE OR YOUNG PERSON WANTING TO ENTER THE INDUSTRY?

Keep an open mind as at graduate level, as you probably don't even know half the jobs available to you or what jobs really involve. What can sound like a glamorous title or company may not always turn out to be that way once you start. I did a placement year at university and that gave me a good grounding in work and also the confidence in applying to jobs when I graduated. I never thought I would end up in IT, but I love project management and if it hadn't been for looking at the attributes of the job rather than my perceptions of IT, I would never have even applied for my first role.

Also, "If you are not happy then move on before it gets you down, as being unhappy is like a dripping tap that will end up causing a flood." My mentor on my graduate scheme gave this advice to me. I've never forgotten it and I have always believed in having a varied career to give me a breadth of experience.

KEY ACCOUNT EXECUTIVE (MEDICAL REPRESENTATIVE) – ALEX HIBBERT

INDUSTRY: Pharmaceutical (Dermatology/Active Cosmetics)
WHAT DOES YOUR ROLE INVOLVE?

Educating clinicians on how our products could benefit/treat their patients. Providing advice and support to the clinicians. Supporting both local and national clinical/educational meetings. Not only do I visit NHS clinicians (Secondary, Primary and Community Care) but I also visit private clinicians. Working with private clinicians is a very different role to working within the NHS. It is more of a 'hard sell' role where you want the customer to actually purchase the product rather than just prescribe the product. Being a medical representative is very different to any other sales role. Particularly within the NHS, it is more about working with the clinicians to enhance their patient care rather than just selling them a product or a service.

WHAT ATTRIBUTES ARE IMPORTANT TO HAVE FOR YOUR JOB?

Excellent planning skills! I cover the whole of Northwest England: Secondary Care, Primary Care and Private Clinics/Hospitals, so it is essential to plan well and know where you need to grow the business and where you need to sustain the business. You need to know what you are doing on a daily basis; otherwise you will just be driving around like a headless chicken. And you always need a back up plan. There is also a lot of admin involved within the role so you need to be able to plan this into your day. Running a territory is basically like running your own business. The only difference being is it also has to fit in with the much wider national and international business.

You have to be thick skinned. Clinicians are very busy people and you hear the word 'no' a lot. You need to be able to handle this and not be deterred by it.

Confidence. There is a lot of presenting involved in being a medical representative, so you need to be able to talk in front of all kinds of audiences. Clinicians also need to have confidence in what you are saying. They have studied and worked extremely hard to get to where they are, so they need to believe and respect what you are saying when you are telling them how your product can help their patients over any of the other competitor products out there.

You need excellent people skills and you need to be able to adapt them to suit the audience. Working with nurses can be very different to working with the consultants, yet they can be just as or sometimes even more important when it comes to getting your product used within a hospital.

HOW DID YOU GET STARTED IN THIS INDUSTRY?
I took a degree in Pharmacology and then I did work experience with a Medial Representative.

WHAT ADVICE WOULD YOU GIVE TO A RECENT GRADUATE OR YOUNG PERSON WANTING TO ENTER THE INDUSTRY?
Make sure you do at least a few days' work experience with a Medical Representative. The job is not for everyone. It can be quite lonely on the road all day and it does involve a lot of driving. Also, because the competition is so high you will not even be interviewed without at least a day's work experience and without having done a lot of research into the role and the NHS.

WHAT'S THE BEST BIT OF ADVICE YOU WERE GIVEN?
If when looking for a job all the positions available say, "at least two years' experience required," ignore it! Apply anyway and do as much research as is physically possible into the role and the NHS. You will surprise the employer with your determination and knowledge (two very important attributes for the job), and even yourself when you are given the role over a lot of experienced people.

MANAGEMENT CONSULTANT/MANAGER – ADAM

INDUSTRY: I consult predominately in Natural Resources (Mining, Oil and Gas)
WHAT DOES YOUR ROLE INVOLVE?
I have many roles within my job as a Management Consultant. I have my day-to-day project where I manage a team of seven who are responsible for successfully transitioning (change

management) a 2,500 workforce from existing processes and systems to a new streamlined and improved way of working. As an executive, I have many roles outside of my project. To name a few, I am accountable for delivering training to junior staff (in Malaysia or Chicago, USA), extra-curricular activities such as leading an Eco Challenge Award to reduce the project's carbon footprint, I run the Triathlon Club and I sit on the performance management team to ensure that our top performers are recognised. And, of course, managing my clients on a day-to-day basis!

WHAT ATTRIBUTES ARE IMPORTANT TO HAVE FOR YOUR JOB?
Establishing and maintaining client relationships is crucial. We work alongside our clients on engagements (usually three – 12 months) so relationships are key to a successful project and outcome.

HOW DID YOU GET STARTED IN THIS INDUSTRY?
I studied business at university and always enjoyed process improvement and change management. That's exactly what I do now for a job!

WHAT ADVICE WOULD YOU GIVE TO A RECENT GRADUATE OR YOUNG PERSON WANTING TO ENTER THE INDUSTRY?
Take your time with your applications to consulting firms. It's a very competitive industry to enter. Take practice case studies online, speak to people already in the industry and do your research.

WHAT'S THE BEST BIT OF ADVICE YOU WERE GIVEN?
Often it's the things that you don't do that you regret and not the things that you do.

FREELANCE JOURNALIST – GEORGIA RICKARD

INDUSTRY: Print, Radio, TV – mostly print.
WHAT DOES YOUR ROLE INVOLVE?
Interviewing all kinds of people – TV stars, experts, regular Jo Blows with interesting opinions, ordinary people with extraordinary stories to tell ... all kinds! Also, looking for stories, staying up-to-date with whatever's going on in the media, and scouring publications for trend-worthy topics.

WHAT ATTRIBUTES ARE IMPORTANT TO HAVE FOR YOUR JOB?
Proactivity! A strong belief in yourself. An ability to be organised, which is necessary for meeting deadlines. Creativity – I'm a features writer, not a news journalist, so for me, it's about telling stories with an angle, not an objective news piece. And, of course, excellent communication skills. You can't be a journalist if you're not a confident and competent writer, speaker and – possibly most important of all – listener.

HOW DID YOU GET STARTED IN THIS INDUSTRY?
I'd studied communications at university, so I had some kind of theoretical background in journalism. When I left my first role at a recruitment agency, I took a short course in writing for magazines, and started picking up the phone, cold-calling editors and selling them story ideas. Some said no, but that was ok – I was used to hearing 'no' from my sales job. I kept reminding myself that J.K. Rowling's *Harry Potter* series was rejected by 12 publishing houses before someone picked up her manuscript – and so, I didn't give up. That's just it – if you want to achieve a dream, you need to believe in yourself before anyone else can or will. Don't give up.

So I kept at it, and I had my first unpaid article published in a free magazine that comes with a gym subscription, called *Fitness First*, within a few weeks. Things snowballed from there. Literally within two months, I was writing feature articles for magazines like *Cosmo*, *CLEO*, *Women's Health* ... and three months after that I was earning enough to move out of my mum's house and support myself (relatively comfortably, too)!

I know that makes it sound easy, but it wasn't – I lived and breathed magazines; I read them every day. I learnt the name of every feature editor, deputy editor, and editor. I learnt their backgrounds, what they had done prior to their roles, I Googled them, followed them on Twitter ... basically, I became a professional stalker! I read every article in the magazines I wanted to work for – even the ones that didn't really interest me. I also got to know freelance writers' names, and noticed who was writing for which magazines, and how often. I studied everyone's writing and noticed different 'voices' of different magazines.

About nine months after I first started freelancing, I met the managing director of the company that publishes *Healthy Food Guide* – and another two months after that I was editing the magazine! I was 23.

It was a huge learning curve – lots of 'thrown in the deep end' experiences, and a whole bunch of reminding myself to fake it till I made it. And I did, I guess. I've just had my first book published – *Weight Training for Dummies* – worked as a government policy advisor on nutrition for the government, hosted regular radio segments on major stations in every metropolitan city in Australia, been interviewed on several national TV programs as an 'expert', been flown to other countries for press trips and to meet with other governments ... lots of stuff. And to think that a few years ago I was wondering if I'd ever be able to be paid to write!

WHAT ADVICE WOULD YOU GIVE TO A RECENT GRADUATE OR YOUNG PERSON WANTING TO ENTER THE INDUSTRY?

Don't give up. Work hard, believe in yourself, follow whatever it is you're passionate about and eventually something will happen for you. Also – get a mentor if you can. Finally, know that things won't fall in your lap. I can't emphasise the 'hard work' part enough.

WHAT'S THE BEST BIT OF ADVICE YOU WERE GIVEN?

Do what makes you happy. Success doesn't lead to happiness – happiness leads to success. Oh, and one more thing – set goals regularly. I set goals for the next day each night before I go to bed, and that really works for me.

ABOUT THE AUTHOR

Emma Vites is a leading careers coach, sales coach and speaker with 8+ years graduate recruitment experience where she has placed and coached graduates into working with some of the leading companies in the world and has ran workshops and presented at City University, UCL, Manchester University and NYU on this topic.

She is the founder of *The Apprentice Project (www. theapprenticeproject.com)* an organisation that coaches graduates and young people on all the skills they need to succeed and she currently works for **LinkedIn**, which is the world's largest professional network. With this experience she can provide valuable insights about how people can use social media to help them secure their dream job.

Emma is a Master NLP practitioner, emotional intelligence coach and IMA practitioner and these tools are taught within 'The graduate bible' to ensure readers learn how to communicate in the most effective way to improve their chances of getting a job considerably.

NOTES:

....

....

....

....

....

....

....

....

....

....

....

....

....

....

....

....

NOTES:

NOTES:

....

....

....

....

....

....

....

....

....

....

....

....

....

....

....

....

NOTES:

NOTES:

....

....

....

....

....

....

....

....

....

....

....

....

....

....

....

....

NOTES:

NOTES:

....

....

....

....

....

....

....

....

....

....

....

....

....

....

....

....

CPSIA information can be obtained
at www.ICGtesting.com
Printed in the USA
LVHW080105090522
718223LV00031B/687

9 781530 311880